INSIDE GAYLAND

INSIDE GAYLAND

RAJESH TALWAR

KALPAZ PUBLICATIONS
Delhi-110052

INSIDE GAYLAND
[*Literature, Law*]

ISBN: 81-7835-015-7

Published in 2001 in India by
Kalpaz Publications
30, Satyawati Nagar
Delhi 110 052
E-Mail: kalpaz@hotmail.com

Laser Typeset at Alphabet, Delhi
Printed at Mehra Offset Printers, New Delhi.

Introduction

The idea of writing this play came to me when as the lawyer for the (ABVA) *AIDS Bhedbhav Virodhi Andolan* I filed a public interest litigation in the High Court of Delhi seeking various reliefs concerned with the control of the spread of AIDS (Acquired Immune Deficiency Syndrome) within the precincts of Tihar jail, New Delhi.

In 1992 at the time when this by now famous ABVA petition was about to be filed, several persons objected to the same. One of the arguments pressed against it raising the question of the constitutionality of Section 377 of the Indian Penal Code was that ABVA was itself not a gay group, so the question arose, whether such a case should be filed by it, at all.

As Dr Paramjit Sahni, one of the senior members of the group however pointed out that, if it meant that Hindus ought not to protest the killings of Sikhs during the 1984 riots and leave it to the Sikhs themselves. Or for example, relating his argument to a more recent context, did it mean that the rest of society should sit silently over the savagery witnessed against Christian nuns in 1999. A second argument raised against the filing was that it might prejudice the Court against the AIDS related mandatory testing of prisoners issue.

At one point during these discussions, I stated that as the advocate on record for the case I would not accept any amendment which amounted to diluting or understating the challenge to Section 377. My undemocratic veto subdued all effective opposition — which was in any case not very substantial, but had only tentatively raised its head — since there was at that point of time practically no lawyer who would take up such a case anyway. Thus it came to be that a crucial connected relief in the petition — which was strenuously opposed by Magsaysay Award winner, Dr Kiran Bedi, who was then Inspector General of Prisons—related to the striking down of Section 377 of the Indian Penal Code.

The petition received a fair amount of publicity in the media including national press and most of our demands made in the petition were, in the course of the litigation, approved of by the Medical Establishment, including NACO (National Aids Control Organization) which was then, and continues to be, the nodal Governmental agency for the AIDS programme in India. It was of course intriguing why they had to wait for the case to be filed before they decided to support us in opposing life endangering policies due to be implemented in Tihar jail.

Be that as it may be, my experiences as a lawyer handling this case, confirmed me in the belief that there was no easy way to tackle mainstream prejudices against individuals, with a different sexual orientation.

As a lawyer with a somewhat literary bent of mind, it occurred to me that it would be an interesting idea to write a play in which the audience would be quite literally put into the shoes of the gay community, and be forced to watch their own reactions and see how conditioned and intolerant they were.

Morality plays are nothing new, but I must confess that I haven't enjoyed most of the ones I've read or watched. However I've certainly enjoyed writing this one! Perhaps it doesn't fit quite exactly into the genre of morality plays, nevertheless I've certainly tried to retain a free tone in it, and keep it from sounding overly didactic. I do believe that as compared with most morality plays, it is considerably more free wheeling in its style and open ended in its conclusions.

When the play was ready, I showed it to ABVA and after a consultation between the members they approved of it and it was brought out during the court case itself in a low price paperback edition which was sold at cost price and used as campaign material. It soon sold itself out.

The play was favorably well received by the gay community, mentioned favorably by several dramatists and theater associations both in India and overseas, favorably reviewed by Bombay Dost and recently extracted in the Seagull Theater Quarterly, possibly the only journal of its kind in India, which comes out from Calcutta.

After a couple of years had passed by, a member of ABVA (who chooses to remain unnamed) suggested to me the possibility of extending the play in order to cover developments subsequent to the admission of the case by the Delhi High Court. I wasn't very sure if this was worthwhile, as I was worried that it might possibly upset the balance and structure of the play.

In 1999, the all but last year of the millennium, the film *Fire* was released, the *Caleri* (Campaign for Lesbian Rights) report came out, and my own *The Third Sex and Human Rights* (Gyan Publishing House, 1999) was released which focusses on the plight of the hijra community in India and compares their situation to that of transsexuals in the West. Besides this there were several other reports and publications such as the Resource Book taken out by Humjinsi, and more importantly, the year was full of campaigns and protests. It was in late 1999 that I began to review my decision about not extending the play, as I felt that here was further material which demanded incorporation within the play, if this could be successfully accomplished. However there was still an ounce of hesitation left about tampering with what had been written during a bout of inspired creativity.

My indecision finally came to an end because of two reasons. Firstly, my publisher said that the play could be published if the length was doubled. This was an undeniable attraction as the play in its earlier avatar had been circulated only in an informal fashion, and had been out of print for more than three years. Seagull Theater Quarterly had overseas subscribers who may have read the extracts, but as yet the journal has a limited readership within the country. All hesitation however came to an end when a well known play director told me after reading the script that the play could be properly staged only if it was extended. In its original form (only half an hour long), it was too short to be staged properly. When increasing traffic, poor road conditions and distances in cities such as Delhi require people to travel sometimes more than an hour to reach a theater, it would be commercially unviable to stage a half hour production. The play had to be at least of one hour duration.

This made sense, and I remembered reading in some book, during my student days, a letter from George Bernard Shaw, the great playwright to Henry James, an equally great novelist, in response to a play the latter had written, that it was by far too short, and a play in order to qualify as a full length play should be of at least eighteen thousand words.

An important suggestion regarding any possible changes (improvement) in the play came from a few friends who felt strongly that in the scene where Kala and Swasthi are sitting in the public park preparing their case, the legal arguments which could actually be used in such a case should have been brought into their conversation.

After much reflection I came to realize that they were right. Having been a practising lawyer for a decade and a half, and having taught in two central universities for six years, I had become so tired and bored with legalese that in the process I had forgotten that had I not been overexposed to legal stimuli, I too might have wanted, indeed required, the play to provide me with a wider legal perspective on various vital arguments, issues and positions connected with the rights of sexual minorities.

While tinkering with this scene with a view to its extension, I decided that I would considerably enhance the scope of the discussion were I to extract and invert the arguments from the relevant paragraphs not only from the ABVA petition but also from landmark judgements delivered by the European Court of Human Rights in the Dudgeon Case (Ser A, No. 45, 4 EHRR 149, 1981) and in Norris (Ser A, No. 142, 13 EHRR 186). To provide balance and scope for dissenting views within the overall context of affirming sexual minority rights, I have also briefly quoted from the judgements in Bowers versus Hardwick, (478 US 186 106 S.Ct. 2841), classified by a prominent writer on legal issues as one of the ten worst ever decisions of the American Supreme Court, together with the judgement upholding slavery. I drew the line at these four cases, one Indian, two European and one American, because while providing a legal perspective was necessary, at the same time I did not want to diminish in any way the overall lightness of the play by overburdening the reader with case law. There are currently more than a hundred connected and relevant judgements from various jurisdictions, notably including Australia, New Zealand, South Africa, Europe and the US.

Plays sometimes require (at least for readers if not a theater audience) explanatory notes, explaining the context more fully to those who may not be aware of it. In this play too it made a lot of sense to add as annexures not only a copy of the original petition filed in the High Court of Delhi by ABVA, but also the full judgement of the European Court of Human Rights in Dudgeon and Norris, two of the cases which are explicitly referred to and quoted from in the body of the play.

The play is not focussed on engendering any great 'understanding' in the sense of talking down to sexual minorities or 'curing' them ; rather the emphasis is on portraying gays as 'People Like Us' (incidentally one of the titles of an ABVA report). Most of us are 'good' people irrespective of our sexual orientations. Some are 'bad'. As they say, with an 'evil' bent of mind. Just as there are heterosexual rapists in society, so also there do exist homosexuals who are rapists. Just as there are heterosexuals who delight in sadism, so also there exist homosexual sadists. To sum up, sexual minorities are neither better nor worse than the rest of us, though a recent study carried out in England came to the conclusion that gay fathers are more caring.

The connected point I wish to raise is that gays too suffer from the same prejudices as the rest in society. Thus, there are gays who look down upon and are prejudiced against bisexuals and dub them as 'traitors' to the cause. Furthermore there are gays and bisexuals who treat transgendered individuals with barely concealed hostility. It is not at all the case that owing to societal oppression sexual minorities will necessarily look to help other disadvantaged sections. This was indeed the case with Siddharth Gautam to whom this book is dedicated, and many other gays as well, but there are also some who will inevitably not hesitate to vent their anger and hate on 'minorities within the minorities' - for instance the hijras.

I hope not to sound pompous, but while the larger and distinct purpose of writing the play is certainly to conscientize the large heterosexual majority in our societies, one of the lesser though significant objectives, in writing this extended version, is to raise the banner of tolerance within the community. Let sexual minorities not squabble amongst themselves and unite to fight intolerance.

Therefore, I found it appropriate to incorporate some reference to the transgendered issue in the play (which has only recently begun raising its legal head in India). In a conversation with Swasthi in Act 1, Scene 4, Kala speaks with Swasthi of the legal problems faced by transgendered individuals. The facts of the XYZ case have been suitably inverted, and the judgement delivered by the European Court of Human Rights has also been included herewith as an annexure in the book, (even though the judgement in that case went against the petitioner) together with the earlier cited judgements on gay rights delivered by that Court.

The play having now been extended to a suitable length (it has crossed by a few thousand the minimum word count standard suggested by GB Shaw) I hope it will find favour with the reading and theater watching public. I trust that a dispassionate reader will find that the purity, humour and flavour of the original has not suffered much. My own view is that these qualities have only been enhanced.

Rajesh Talwar

DRAMATIS PERSONAE

Swasthi
Sangeeta, *Swasthi's wife*

Kenneth, *a spaceship driver*
Mela Malani, *a Senior Advocate, Supreme Court of Gayland*
Kala, *her junior*
Jack, *a Justice of High Court of Gayland*

Alif Bachpan, *a filmstar*
Lekha, *a filmstar*

Virender, *a Station House Officer*
Vivek, *a Constable*

Geeta, *a young collegiate lesbian*
Phulwa, *Geeta's lover, a middle-aged human rights activist*

Balam, *a male homosexual*
Navneet, *Balam's lover*

Shanney, *a male heterosexual poet*
Yani, *a journalist from* Vista News, *a highly regarded news channel*
A photojournalist, clerks and typists in Mela Malani's *office. The Court clerk, peshkar, etc., in the High Court of Gayland, a TV technician and some constables.*

ACT ONE

Scene I

The House of Swasthi

Sangeeta, *an attractive, dark complexioned housewife in her late twenties, dressed in a cotton sari is sitting on a sofa in the drawing-room, with an untitled book in her hand. All at once she stands up and assuming a theatrical pose, begins to read out extracts from the book to a non-existent audience*[1].

Sangeeta : *(In a passionate tone)*
'Her body bristling with longing,
Her breath sucking in words of confusion
Her voice cracking in deep cold fear-
Obsessed by intense thoughts of passion,
Radhika sinks in a sea of erotic mood,
Clinging to you in her meditation, cheat!
She ornaments her limbs
When a leaf quivers or a feather falls.
Suspecting your coming
She spreads out the bed[2]
(she pauses momentarily and resumes in a sad voice)
'And waits long in meditation
Making her bed or ornaments and fantasies,
She evokes a hundred details of you
In her own graceful play.
But the frail girl will not survive
Tonight without you.[3]

(She picks up a cap from the table, puts it on, and resumes her speech, now striking a masculine demeanour)

'Fretful Radha, don't suspect me!
A rival has no place
When your voluptuous breasts and hips
Always occupy my heart.
Only the ghost of love is potent enough
To penetrate my subtle core.

When I start to press your heavy breasts
Fulfill our destined rite!
Punish me, lovely fool
Bite me with your cruel teeth!
Chain me with your creeper arms!
Crush me with your hard breasts!
Angry Goddess, don't weaken with joy
Let Love's despised arrows
Pierce me to sap my life's power.[4]

Pauses here, flips through the text, and resumes

Your moist lips glow
Like crimson autumn blossoms;
The skin of your cheek
Is a honey-coloured flower.
Fierce Radha, your eyes glower
Like gleaming dark lotuses;
Your nose is a sesame flower;
Your teeth are white jasmine.
Love's flower arms conquer worlds
By worshipping your face.[5]

She pauses here, refers to the book, then breaks out in speech again, striking the same somewhat masculine pose.

'My heart values his vulgar ways,
Refuses to admit my rage,
Feels strangely elated,
And keeps denying his guilt.
When he steals away without me
To indulge his craving
For more young women,
My perverse heart
Only wants Krishna back.
What can I do?'[6]

(The bell rings just then. The door is pushed open)

Enter Swasthi, *a short-statured, balding man in his early thirties, fair, with a moustache. He is wearing black trousers, a white shirt, a black coat, and has a lawyer's white band tied around his collar. He enters, and immediately collapses on the sofa.*

Swasthi : Oh, I'm so tired!

Sangeeta : *(She has an annoyed expression on her face)* So? Did you make any money today?

Swasthi : The client has promised to pay me the next time.

Sangeeta : *(Angrily)* Is there ever a next time? I've been hearing 'next time' since the day I got married.

Swasthi : Darling, can I have a cup of tea?

Sangeeta : *(Sullenly)* There is no milk.

Swasthi : Then will you please make me some black coffee. I've had a long, hard day at the Court today.

Sangeeta : Coffee? Don't you know that coffee is at least three, four times as expensive as tea *(Turns to the audience)* Coffee, he says. Hah! You're like Marie Antoinette, wife of Louis VI, who was hanged. When the people complained of lack of bread, she said very smartly, 'In that case, why don't they eat cakes?'

Swasthi : I can have some lemon tea in that case.

Sangeeta : *(Angrily)* There are no lemons either, nor is there any sugar (*pause*) and there are no tea leaves either.

Swasthi : *(Changing the subject)* You are looking very beautiful today.

Sangeeta : *(Scornfully)* Hah! He says I look beautiful. *(Telling the audience)* Can I look beautiful in such an old sari? Now that it's winter, all the women in the neighbourhood are out in their silks, and only poor old I have to keep coming out like this. *(Gestures at the sari she is wearing)* And even this, this blasted cotton sari, you gave me two years ago! *(Looks tearful now)*

Swasthi : *(Consolingly)* I'll buy a new sari on your birthday this time, my dear, I promise.

Sangeeta : *(Sniffing)* And what will you buy this time? Some more cotton?

Swasthi : No, no, I will buy a beautiful Kanjeevaram sari for you. Would you like that?

Sangeeta : *(Eagerly)* Really?

Swasthi : Yes, of course. Not that you need it, my dear. You look beautiful anyhow.

Sangeeta : You lawyers never give up, do you? As if I don't know what you want. Don't try and change the subject. And don't you try and come close to me. I am not in the mood.

Swasthi : Are you ever in the mood?

Sangeeta : Not until you start making some money.

Swasthi : Listen, I am going to make some money very soon.

Sangeeta : Oh, I have heard that one before. Don't try and fool me.

Swasthi : No, I mean it seriously. Why don't you believe me? There is a chance now.

Sangeeta : *(Eagerly now)* What is it?

Swasthi : I am going to outerspace.

Sangeeta : Outerspace! To a different planet! Great! Fantastic! When did this happen? Where are you going?

Swasthi : There was this cultural exchange programme for young lawyers organised by the Ministry of External Affairs. I had applied a few months ago. Out of two thousand lawyers I am the only one to have been selected. I have to leave day after tomorrow.

Sangeeta : *(Upset)* Oh! and what will happen to my Kanjeevaram sari which you just promised to buy on my birthday.

Swasthi : I will get your Kanjeevaram, dearest, Don't worry about that. It's only a month-long programme. I'll be back the day before your birthday.

Sangeeta : Mind you don't miss your flight. I wouldn't put it past you to do that. Or you might just keep sleeping during the flight and reach some other planet.

Swasthi : This will not happen, Sangeeta, my dear. Just don't worry. *(Trying to cheer her up)* In fact I'll get you some clothes from this planet as well. I don't know what the women there wear, of course.

Sangeeta : *(Enthusiastically)* Get a few pieces of whatever they wear. It will be exotic and much better than what is available in the boutiques in Hauz Khas village, where Mrs Sharma, our neighbour, gets her clothes from. All the women in the colony will eat their hearts out when they learn that what I am wearing is from outerspace.

Swasthi : I have to train with a leading criminal lawyer from that planet. It's a lady called Mela Malani.

Sangeeta : Never heard of such a name. What a strange name *(Repeats it, rolling her tongue)* Mela Malani! Which planet are you going to?

Swasthi : It's a very ancient planet called Gayland.

Sangeeta : Gayland! *(Puzzled)* Never heard of that name either.

Swasthi : We didn't know of the existence of this planet till recently. In fact the galaxy itself has been discovered very recently. E-mail links were established hardly a year ago, and outerspace flights have commenced by the two-seater Shuttle spacecraft only four months ago. There is very little we know of their customs and practices.

Sangeeta : It may take you some time to adjust to their food. They will probably have a different religion over there as well.

Swasthi : The term for it is 'cultural shock'. At the briefing today at the consulate, they spoke of the sometimes severe mental and emotional adjustments a person has to make when he visits a new planet.

Sangeeta : *(Understandingly)* And when you have adjusted to their way of doing things, and you come back to our planet, then you will have to readjust to how things are done here.

Swasthi : That's very intelligent of you, my dear. As a matter of fact, you're perfectly right. They have a term for that as well. Reverse culture shock

Sangeeta : Reverse culture shock! Oh, that's interesting!

Swasthi : Some astronomers had spoken of having sighted the galaxy decades ago; but their findings had been dismissed by later scientists who called them cranks. Now with communication links actually established, it's clearly established that the earlier ones were right and the later ones wrong.

Sangeeta : That's like the babyfood controversy. Every few years they change their minds about whether or not it's good for babies. What is this galaxy called?

Swasthi : Just as our galaxy is known as the Milky Way, this one is known as the Pink Way. You of course wouldn't know about it, my dear wife, but it's been coming out in the paper everyday.

Sangeeta : *(Musing)* The Pink Way! What a beautiful name, don't you think so? This reminds me, when you buy dresses from Gayland, buy me a nice blouse in shocking pink, will you? For some reason they've run out of this colour at the market. It's not available anywhere.

Swasthi : All right.

Sangeeta : Isn't it amazing how God has created all these wonderful galaxies and planets for us to visit.

Swasthi : I'm not so sure if God created them for us to visit.

Sangeeta : *(Miffed)* What do you know of God's motives, may I ask? Have you read a religious book in your life? You know only of law books, but I have read the higher law.

Swasthi : *(Placatingly)* That is quite true, my dear wife. And what have you been reading these days?

Sangeeta : *(Proudly)* I've just finished reading Jayadev's *Gitagovinda*.

Swasthi : That's interesting! (Shakes his head in amazement) What next, what next?

Sangeeta : *(Piously)* Next, I will be reading the *Bible*. Although all religions say the same thing, there are still some differences in their approach. (a thought crosses her mind) Tell me, why couldn't you have been chosen to go to a more respectable and well-known planet? Something like Pluto or Neptune? This sounds like a third world planet. *(Turns cheerful)*

Anyway, outerspace is outerspace. You will have the stamp of being an outerspace returned when you get back.

Swasthi : Moreover, I will probably be able to save a lot of money on this trip by staying in cheaper hotels.

Sangeeta : Yes. You can get me some perfumes and cosmetics as well. I haven't got any left now. I'll give you a list. But take care of yourself. I don't trust this woman a bit. Mela Malani or whatever her name is. Come closer. Why are you sitting so far away? *(They are sitting on the bed now. She gives him a hug)* When did you say you would be coming back?

Swasthi : After one month. *(Switches off the light).*

ACT TWO

Scene I

The market place in Gayland

(Moving from one end to the other, this set has a spaceship landing centre, a cinema hall and a restaurant. Swasthi lands in Gayland, his escort hands him the money and disappears. He then walks ahead to a cinema hall, where he asks for directions to Mela Malani's office, and when he is unsuccessful in finding out the location, walks ahead to a restaurant named 'Gaylord' where he makes enquiries from the manager).

Kenneth : *(The space shuttle driver)* Hey, are you asleep or something? Come on out. We have landed.

Swasthi : *(Sleepily)* Where am I?

Kenneth : *(Impatiently)* You're in Gayland, that's where you are. *(An idea occurs to him)* Hey, aren't you supposed to be a lawyer?

Swasthi : *(Looking bedraggled)* Yes, that's right.

Kenneth : *(Looks him up and down disbelievingly)* Amazing! Simply amazing!

Swasthi : *(Yawns)* Why is my being a lawyer that surprising?

Kenneth : I mean you don't look like one.

Swasthi : What do lawyers look like?

Kenneth : Search me. *(To the audience, in a stage whisper)* Like vultures, or something? *(Turns back to Swasthi)* Well, come on out my friend, whoever you are.

Swasthi : *(Steps out of the shuttle sleepily)* What's the great hurry, my good man?

Kenneth : There is a hurry. I've got to go off to Mars now, and then to Venus. I'm already running behind schedule.

Swasthi : *(Looks at his watch)* Why did we get delayed?

Kenneth : *(Repeats, sourly)* Why did we get delayed? Why do Court cases get delayed, you tell me that. Get yourself another escort next time if you're all that fussy.

(Shakes his head in disapproval) Amazing! Simply amazing!

Swasthi : *(Appeasingly)* I wasn't making a complaint, my friend. I only wanted to know the reason. It was engine trouble perhaps?

Kenneth : *(Mollified)* Oh! I see. Well, I couldn't see very clearly the last few hours of the flight. That's because it was early morning.

Swasthi : *(Understanding)* So there was fog?

Kenneth : No, that wasn't it.

Swasthi : *(Correcting himself)* I meant smog actually. There's plenty of that in Delhi too these days. *(Looks around)* But it's all cleared up now, hasn't it?

Kenneth : *(Annoyed)* No, no that wasn't it. Mornings are a bad time to land in Gayland because there is a pinkish haze all around the planet for several hundreds of miles, so you can't actually see very clearly and make out where exactly the planet is, because this planet, you see, is pink....and it's very small.

Swasthi : Pink! The planet is pink?

Kenneth : Yes. Just like Mars is red, and Earth is brown. The ground—what you call earth on your planet—is pink. Amazing, isn't it?

Swasthi : *(Looks at the floor, which is pink)* Yes. So it is.

Kenneth : Here is a packet for you containing your return ticket and money for expenses over here.

Swasthi : How much is it?

Kenneth : Oh, about twenty thousand purees.

Swasthi : Purees?

Kenneth : Yes, that's what the local currency is called.

Swasthi : Would you by any chance know how much it is worth.

Kenneth : How much is twenty thousand purees worth? Well, twenty thousand purees exactly. Not a puree less, not a puree more. Count them, if you don't trust me.

Swasthi : No sir, what I meant to say was do you have any idea about the inter-planetary currency exchange rate?

Kenneth : Oh, I see what you mean. Wait, let me check. *(Takes out a small chart, and examines it)* Yes, here it is. You're in luck. There is a very favourable exchange rate for you here. Two purees are worth ten rupees. Let me check with my calculator. *(Takes out a pocket calculator and does some sums with it)* Yes, each puree is worth five rupees, which means that twenty thousand purees are worth... *(Does his sums with the calculator once again)* yes, I have it, they are worth one hundred thousand rupees. Oh! that's a lot of money in your part of the world. Isn't it?

Swasthi : Yes, indeed it is, Mr. Escort. Thank you very much, sir.

Kenneth : Not at all. Now make sure you are on time on the day of your departure because there are only two flights a month from this place to where you come from.

Swasthi : Oh, I'll be on time! I have to return in time for my wife's birthday, otherwise she'll skin me alive.

Kenneth : Is that what wives do on that planet of yours? Amazing!

Swasthi : Listen, that was just a figure of ...

Kenneth : *(Pokes Swasthi's behind with a finger).* Take care of this while you are here. They do things a little differently here you know.

Swasthi : I don't understand what you mean.

Kenneth : Well, I don't have any time to explain. I told you

I'm in a hurry *(Climbs back into the spaceship)* Have a good time anyhow. I'm off.

Swasthi : Bye bye, Mr. Escort. It was nice meeting you.

(*Exit* Kenneth)

Swasthi : *(To himself)* This woman Mela Malani hasn't even sent anyone to receive me at the landing centre. I wonder if there is any cheap lodging where I can stay and save some money. Perhaps Mela Malani is willing to give me a small room in her home to stay in. But, first of all let me change my dress. What should I wear now? Where's that blasted Lonely Planet Rough Guide to Gayland. *(Rummages in his bag, and takes out a tattered copy of the book)* Yes, this is it. *(Flips through the pages)* Here it is. *(Reads aloud)* "The favourite dress of the pink planet, as it is popularly known, is the national dress worn by all and sundry and is red and white. Red for revolution; white for purity. A combination of Karl Marx and Mahatma Gandhi, not that these people would ever realize it." *(Rummages in his bag again and takes out a red shirt)* Red shirt! *(Takes out a pairs of trousers)* White trousers! I'm sure I'll make a big hit with these people once I am seen wearing their favourite colour. Now where do I have a bath and change into these clothes? *(Espies a changing room)* That's the place. *(Turns to the audience)* Just excuse me a moment ladies and gentlemen. I won't be long. *(Gives the attendant outside the cloakroom some money, enters the toilet, and closes the door behind him)*

(Enter Phulwa, a middle-aged human rights activist, and Geeta, her teenage collegiate lover. They go and stand outside the cinema hall.)

Phulwa : I told you the show started at 3.30 and not 3 O'clock.

Geeta : The papers misprinted the timing. Never mind, dear, we have to wait only for another half-an-hour.

Phulwa : Why have we come to see this movie, *Janam*?

Geeta : Why? What's wrong, dear? Don't you like the cast?

Phulwa : It's not the cast I mind. It's the story. It's the same old stereotyped romance. Both these guys are football stars, top scorers and they are to play this match representing rival teams. During the course of this match they fall in love. I wonder why our film makers can't be more experimental. You have seen one, you have seen them all.

Geeta : I don't know. I like these movies. At least this one is light and entertaining. And it's a got good music. Who wants to go and see one of those art movies? I mean they are artistic, but they can be so slow and boring.

Phulwa : My dear, you need to develop your taste in good cinema. It's a pity that you've been going around with me for so long, and yet I haven't been able to influence you in this regard.

Geeta : Maybe you're right. Let's go and see this film about a man having a relationship with a woman. I've seen it once, but I don't mind seeing it again.

Phulwa : *(Outraged)* What? You want to skip meaningful cinema and go and see that perverted film.

Geeta : Well, yes. At least it's an interesting film.

Phulwa : You find it interesting. I find it perverted.

Geeta : You know sometimes I think you're such an obscurantist. I sometimes wonder how you happen to be an activist of the Democratic Rights Organisation.

Phulwa : *(Proudly)* I'm an old timer, one of the most senior members.

Geeta : That's what attracted me to you in the beginning. I remember the day you came to our college to lecture on human rights. It was on my birthday. I turned sixteen that day.

Phulwa : *(Sentimentally)* And then we went for coffee...

Geeta : Obviously you don't seem to consider heterosexual rights a human right.

Phulwa : Yes, I think all this talk of heterosexual rights under the garb of human rights is actually giving human rights itself a bad name. There is so much of poverty and unemployment on this planet. And police repression. These issues are not important. They only concern the debauched elite of our society.

Geeta : That's not true at all. Haven't you read the Kinsley report? If you consider the figures given in that report there must be hundreds of thousands of heterosexuals on this planet.

Phulwa : Who knows of the authenticity of these reports? What is their basis?

Geeta : *(Loudly)* Who knows about the authenticity of your reports, may I ask? You turn up your nose with a superior air whenever anyone in the media questions you on the figures you've given in your last report regarding police excesses.

Phulwa : *(Frustrated)* What are you trying to say?

Geeta : Listen, I wholeheartedly support all your activities, but can't you see that your vision is very narrow, and overtly puritanical.

Phulwa : You know the trouble with you is that you have too open a mind.

Geeta : What's wrong with having an open mind?

Phulwa : *(Laughs)* It's liable to have a lot of rubbish thrown in. I really think you're too liberal...

Geeta : And I think you're semi-fascist. All your democratic rights talk is a lot of hot air. What's wrong with this movie they showed the other day?

Phulwa : *Aag*. You mean *Aag*, the fire, don't you?

Geeta : Yes, that's right. I thought it was a damn fine movie.

Phulwa : I thought it was sick. In fact I happened to see it just by accident. I had gone to this friend's place for an evening cocktail and someone at the party had managed to get hold of the cassette in those days when the Government of Gayland had banned it, so there was a lot of general curiousness about it, and someone suggested we watch it, so we all sat and watched all three hours of it.

Geeta : What did you think?

Phulwa : I thought it was downright stupid. I'm sure the movie would have flopped badly if it hadn't been for the ban which they lifted later. I mean, it's such an implausible story line. Two women married to each other for many years, and one of them is being neglected by the other. Being denied of any sexual relief because of the other's celibacy vows. So does this mean that this neglected spouse, what's her name, Rita isn't it? Should she suddenly start having sex with a man! I mean, come on, for God's sake, if her spouse wasn't giving her sex, she could have gone to another woman. Her spouse was not the last woman on the planet, was she?

Geeta : Well, even I found that situation somewhat unrealistic, I must admit. It would have been far better if she hadn't tried to make out that a woman might turn to a man — or the other way around for that matter — if she wasn't getting sexual satisfaction from her spouse.

Phulwa : Exactly! The perverted women who actually like to have sex with men do so because that's how they are, not because they couldn't find fulfilment in a normal, healthy relationship with another woman.

Geeta : You know, I don't fully agree with you there. I think this might actually be the case in a few cases but by and large what you say is true. In fact, I actually know a couple of very attractive ladies teaching in my school who have been rumoured to have been having it off with the male Principal who is a well-known pervert. Mind you, they are both very attractive, so it isn't as if they couldn't find other women to have a relationship with. It's just that's how they seem to prefer it. One of them confided to me that she's been like this since childhood.

Phulwa : I don't know why you talk to these perverts.

Geeta : You're so conservative, Phulwa. I don't know how we happen to be lovers, our thinking is so different.

Phulwa : I think it's because of movies like *Aag* that all these problems arise. It's the movies and the media which contribute no end to these ills.

Geeta : No, it's the other way round, silly. The movies reflect what actually happens in real life. In a way, I appreciate what the director of the film tried to do. By showing that the woman turned to a man only after she had suffered rejection from her own sex, the film sounded more plausible and the theme more acceptable. If she had shown a woman actually preferring to go with a man without having had any problems in her marriage to another woman, then the conservative public would have gone mad. They would have actually burnt the cinema halls down.

Phulwa : Well, there were strong and legitimate protests...

Geeta : Not legitimate at all. Just some goons from that right wing conservative party who tried to disrupt some shows.. I mean, how can you stop people from seeing a film if they want to?

Phulwa : Didn't the heterosexual activists stand outside the theatre after the ban was lifted with their slogans and posters?

Geeta : Yes, but that was so peaceful. Those goons just smashed the window panes. Reactionary bastards!

Phulwa : That's true, I agree with you. But when you talk like this, I sometimes think . . . *(Hesitates)*

Geeta : Go on. Say it. Why do you stop?

Phulwa : I sometimes think that you might also have a heterosexual streak in you.

Geeta : *(Challengingly)* And if I do? *(Angrily)* Come on, Phulwa. You insult me. Do you think I support the heterosexuals only because I myself am a heterosexual. That's terrible. How can you say that? You oppose this new anti-terrorism law, don't you? Is that because you yourself are a terrorist?

Phulwa : *(Appeasingly)* All I'm saying is that I believe all such movies, or plays for that matter, should be banned. They are simply not good for public morality.

Geeta : *(Putting her hands on her hips aggressively)* And you, Madam Phulwa, as the self-appointed guardian of public morality are going to decide for the people of Gayland what is right and what is wrong. Is that it?

Phulwa : Listen, I'm only repeating what our great thinker and revolutionist King Sol said when he banned illegal and unnatural practices.

Geeta : *(Sarcastically)* So you, Madam Phulwa, are the successor to King Sol himself.

Phulwa : I don't mean to say that. But do you mean to say, dear Geeta, that you don't agree with what King Sol wrote.

Geeta : Well, I don't disagree with everything he said; but, sure, I think he made some mistakes.

Phulwa : Mistakes? King Sol made mistakes, and you, Madam Geeta, as the self-appointed guardian of public morality are out to correct those mistakes!

Geeta : Touche! But seriously Phulwa, you can't accept what King Sol said as being infallible. That's religious fundamentalism. One has to see things in a wider perspective. His teachings have to be interpreted according to the times we live in. What he said five hundred years ago, or what some other prophet might have said two thousand years ago, cannot be unstintingly accepted today. There are many of the teachings of King Sol which must be seen in this context. It was right of him to have taken such harsh views on heterosexuality during his times, because there was the threat of famines and diseases due to population explosion. Today we need have no such fears.

Phulwa : And therefore we should promptly abandon whatever our forefathers have said or written, and allow the new generation to see whatever trashy material these wretched perverts come up with.

Geeta : No, you would rather suffocate their minds and not even let people breathe. I'm beginning to feel suffocated myself.

Phulwa : And since I, your lady lover am suffocating you so badly as you just disclosed, why don't you just go and get involved in a heterosexual relationship just like the heroine of the movie did?

Geeta : Why do you have to react so violently to everything I say?

Phulwa : It's because you talk such nonsense! As you know there is a law which provides that when people are involved in heterosexual relationships they contravene the criminal law of the land and can be sentenced to a term in prison.

Geeta : Of course I know. I read the papers too. Besides, you mean the Alif and Lekha case, don't you? The whole planet has been discussing the case. Everyone knows about it. As a matter of fact there is a big demonstration planned outside the Courtroom on the day they appear for their trial.

Phulwa : *(Excitedly)* That's exactly my point! Don't you see the tremendous contradiction which all the media and the newspapers have completely missed? The point is that when you have this law, Section 377 of the Gayland Penal Code, which makes it a crime for a person to have a heterosexual relationship, then how can you permit the screening of movies where the main story concerns one such relationship. Don't you see the contradiction?

Geeta : I do, but not in the way you see it perhaps. There is a contradiction but that doesn't mean that movies like these should be banned.

Phulwa : Then?

Geeta : It simply means, you blockhead, that Section 377 of the Gayland Penal Code should be scrapped as being otiose, void and unconstitutional as well as being violative of the fundamental rights of the people of Gayland.

Phulwa : *(Angry)* You've picked all these expressions from those stupid liberal newspapers, haven't you? Do you mean to say that you actually support Alif and Lekha in what they did?

Geeta : *(Loudly)* Yes, I do! For your information I mean to join the demonstration outside the Courtroom this coming Monday.

Phulwa : *(Agitated)* You never turn up for our demonstrations and you want to go there. You can't go there. People may see you. What will they think? They might think that you're also a heterosexual.

Geeta : *(Angry)* That's the least of my concerns. I'm going to go, even if it means facing arrest or a lathi charge. I'd like to see who's going to stop me! *(In tears now)* And if you, Madam Phulwa, can't accept this then you'll just have to lump it, or we can just call off this relationship.

Phulwa : *(in a pacifying tone)* Now, who's reacting violently? *(Gives Geeta a handkerchief)* I'm sorry. It's not important at all. Go demonstrate wherever you like. *(Repeats)* I'm truly sorry, Geeta.

Geeta : *(Smiling through her tears)* That's more like it.

Phulwa : Give me a kiss now.

Geeta : No, you give me a kiss.

They begin smooching.

(Swasthi has completed his toilet. Even while Geeta and Phulwa were having this argument, Swasthi opens the toilet door after having changed into the red shirt and white trousers, and facing a mirror and wash basin, begins a leisurely shave, and combing of his hair. At this juncture in the scene, he has just finished his toilet and is ready to leave.)

Swasthi : Now how do I find out where she lives? *(Sees the cinema hall)* Oh, I know where to ask, I will go to that cinema hall and ask around. Somebody is bound to know where such a famous lawyer lives. *(Starts walking towards the cinema hall).*

(When he reaches the cinema hall, he goes to see the posters and is quite shocked. One poster has the movie titled 'Playing Ball' and has a picture of two men in football shorts, holding a football in their hands and looking lovingly into each other's, eyes. Another poster shows two women ice-skating in a rink arm in arm and the movie is titled 'Romance on Wheels'. He then spots Phulwa and Geeta and goes to enquire from them. They are busy gazing into each other's, eyes lovingly.)

Swasthi : *(Interrupting them hesitantly)* Excuse me, ladies. Can you tell me where Ms. Mela Malani's office is?

Geeta : Get lost. Who cares where she lives? Can't you see we're busy?

(They kiss again. Swasthi moves away, and goes over to Balam, who is standing alone nearby, is wearing a ring in one ear and who has been watching him eagerly.)

Swasthi : Good afternoon, Sir.

Balam : Good afternoon, buddy. Since when did politicians start speaking the language of the common man.

Swasthi : *(Indignantly)* I am not a politician. What makes you imagine that I am one?

Balam : *(Raises his eyebrows)* No? Well, sorry, but you can't blame me for thinking so. It's only politicians who wear red and white these days.

Swasthi : *(Haughtily)* I'm a visitor from Earth. I have learnt that this is your national dress, which everyone takes great pride in.

Balam : *(Chuckles)* National dress! Which everyone is proud of? *(Laughs heartily)* Listen to me, my friend. You have come late by at least fifty years. Fifty years ago people did feel some pride in red and white. Now only criminals and politicians wear this dress. You say you're from another planet. I can see what must have happened. Have you heard the story about the politician and the nudist camp?

Swasthi : No, I haven't. I told you I'm new around these parts. Besides, I'm not a politician.

Balam : *(Enjoying himself)* Yes, I can see that now, but you can listen to a story, can't you? The story is that there is this well known politician in this city who was invited to a nudist camp not very far from here.

Swasthi : Why are you telling me this story?

Balam : Just listen. He reaches this nudist camp completely naked, out of respect for their sentiments.

Swasthi : *(Smiles)* That's funny!

Balam : Wait. You haven't heard the punch line yet. The nudist camp's welcoming committee members had all worn clothes because he was coming.

Swasthi : That's a very funny story, but I can't really see what it has to do with me, or my dress.

Balam : I can see that you don't see. *(Explains)* I was just trying to chat you up my dear.

Swasthi : I don't understand you at all, Sir. But now that I have listened to your joke, and a very fine joke it was I can assure you, could you please guide me to the office of Ms. Mela Malani, Senior Advocate?

Balam : Listen, sweetheart. Why do you want to go and meet that lawyer? Don't have anything to do with lawyers. They will suck you dry. If you've got a problem, I'll help you *(Obviously fancies Swasthi)*.

Swasthi : No, no. You don't understand. I need to meet her as part of a inter-governmental culture exchange programme.

Balam : *(Shrugs)* I'm afraid I don't know where she lives. I have got a clean record. I have never been accused of any crime. *(Rhetorically)* Why should I know where she lives? *(Points out to a building)* See that hotel. It's written 'Gaylord' outside it. It's a very old and established lodging house, with a restaurant on the ground floor. It's been there since before my birth. Go and enquire inside. Ask the proprietor, a Mr. Bhumbha. He is sure to know.

Swasthi : *(Effusive)* Thank you. Thank you very much.

(Swasthi walks to the hotel. Hotel Gaylord is a fairly imposing structure and the restaurant on the ground floor which Swasthi enters is a plush, red-carpeted affair. Inside are sitting two poets, one male and one female, on different tables looking out of the window, facing the audience. At the rear end, you have cabins covered by a curtain with a board outside saying 'Families only'. This naturally means either a girl couple or male couple, with or without children. A man and a woman together have to sit outside in the main part of the restaurant.)

Maya : This is not a very original idea, Shanney.
Shanney : Protest poetry? Of course it's nothing new. It's probably as old as poetry itself.
Maya : No, I meant performance poetry. That too has been done before.
Shanney : I know that! However I don't think it's been done in the style we've planned. Most of it has been solo till now. This will be the first duet.
Maya : Should we start?
Shanney : Yes. You first.

Enter Swasthi
(The poets start flinging their hands about, and singing love poems. After reciting two lines, the male poet breaks off and the female continues. In this way, they both complete their poems.)
Maya : This hateful society has chained our souls...
Shanney : Not letting us live according to our desires...
Maya : It has invaded the privacy...
Shanney : Of our bedrooms...
Maya : And dictates to us...
Shanney : Not only whom we shall love...
Maya : And whom we shall not love...
Shanney : But also how we shall make love.
Maya : They have already made loving a crime...
Shanney : Why can't I love or make love...
Maya : To a man...
Shanney : And I to a woman?
Maya : Soon they shall impose...
Shanney : Taxes...

Maya : On hard ones.

Swasthi : *(Passes by these poets with a bewildered expression on his face and goes to the manager).* Are you Mr. Bhumbha?

Bhumbha : Yes, I am.

Swasthi : Excuse me, Sir. Is this a hotel?

Bhumbha : What does it look like to you?

Swasthi : Can I ask what are the room charges for a night?

Bhumbha : I'm afraid we're all booked up for the moment. What was it you wanted? A double, or a single room?

Swasthi : A single.

Bhumbha : I might just be able to squeeze one out for you. But mind you, we are a straight decent place. I don't want any guys going up to your room late in the night. A single will cost you five hundred purees a day.

Swasthi : *(protests)* That's two thousand five hundred rupees! Why that's daylight robbery! What is this, a five-star hotel?

Bhumbha : It's the oldest and the most respectable lodging house in the city, son. Let me tell you that you aren't going to find anything better in this price. You want to stay in one of the deluxe hotels, it won't cost you less than one thousand five hundred purees a night. You want to stay in a one of the cheap places, you'll end up spending more on your doctor getting rid of the skin infections you'll contract from the linen. See those certificates hanging on the wall. They're given by the Tourist Authority, and they all say that Gaylord Hotel is the very best that Gayland can boast of. Like I told you, we're all booked out, but seeing you looking kind of lost and presumably a foreigner in these parts, I thought that may be I could squeeze a small room out for you, but you have to commit right now or it will be booked up as well.

Swasthi : Can I perhaps request you to hold that room for me for just one hour?

Bhumbha : You want to go and check out the other places? Haven't I told you it'll be a waste of your time?

Swasthi : No, no, you don't understand. I'm a trainee lawyer from another planet. I have to spend some days working with Mela Malani, the famous lawyer. It is possible that she may have made arrangements for me to stay somewhere.

Bhumbha : Oh, well, in that case, all right. *(Looks at his watch)* An hour from now, did you say? I won't hold it a minute longer, please understand that.

Swasthi : Yes, yes, can you now please tell me how I could reach Ms. Mela Malani's office?

Bhumbha : Walk straight ahead. At the crossing turn right, then left, then right. First house round the corner. Have you got that right? Right, left, right.

Swasthi : *(In a bit of a daze, repeats)* Right, left, right.

(*Exit* Swasthi)

ACT TWO

Scene II

The Office of Ms. Mela Malani

(Kala, Mela Malini's *junior is sitting on her senior's chair, talking to herself)*

Kala : *(Talking to herself)* One of these days, very soon I shall be sitting on this chair and I shall have my junior sitting over there (points at a table and chair in the corner where she normally sits). Of course I won't treat my junior as badly as she treats me. I will be fair and square. I will give her a decent sum of money every month so that she can manage her affairs quite well. I will be a more successful, better lawyer than she is. She doesn't even know how to treat clients. She is so snooty. I won't be like that ...

so that the clients will have a lot of respect for me. Now supposing I was sitting here and a client were to call ...

Swasthi : *(Standing outside the office)* This seems to be the place. There is a board outside which says Mela Malani, Senior Advocate. I think I shall press the bell *(Presses the switch).*

Kala : *(From inside, in a welcoming tone)* Come in.

(Enter Swasthi *carrying a battered suitcase and holdall.)*

Swasthi : *(Nervously)* Excuse me. Are you Ms. Mela Malani?

Kala : No, I'm afraid not. She works with me. I am *(Clears her throat)* associated with her. I am the person who actually does most of the work. I have become such an expert, Sir, that I can now make out a client's problem by just looking at him. *(Pauses)* Now let me guess. You have been fired from your job and want to raise an industrial dispute.

Swasthi : No.

Kala : I didn't think so. Do you have a matrimonial problem with your spouse?

Swasthi : No. Of course not.

Kala : *(Impatiently)* Well, then what is it?

Swasthi : I knew it! I was just going to say that! (pauses) So what is it you want?

Kala : I have to work as a trainee...

(Enter Ms. Mela Malani *in a swirl of robes followed in a servile fashion by two assistants, carrying loads of law books and reports in their arms.* Mela Malani *notices* Kala *sitting on her chair and freezes her with a glance.* Kala *immediately gets up with a guilty expression and walks back to her table and chair in the corner.* Ms. Malani *occupies her seat.)*

Mela : *(Addresses Swasthi briskly)* Yes. What can I do for you?

Swasthi : Madam, I have come from Earth ...

Mela : I see. You are the trainee. Welcome to Gayland. I hope you had a comfortable journey. Where are you staying?

Swasthi : *(Nervously)* I haven't thought of that as yet. Could you suggest a place, Mà'am?

Mela : There is absolutely no space in my house otherwise, you could have stayed there. (Thinks for a while) You could stay at the Gaylòrd hotel perhaps. It's not far from here and the rates are quite reasonable. Now, can I see your papers?

*(*Swasthi *digs into various coat pockets, finally manages to find the pages in his trouser pocket and hands them over to her.)*

Mela : Hmm. *(Checking various papers)* Yes. These papers seem to be in order. Now, when would you like to begin work?

Swasthi : Whenever you say, Ma'am.

Mela : In that case why not start today? Start immediately, as a matter of fact. I will give you a case right now, which you and Kala can prepare together. *(Shouts)* Kala!

Kala : Yes, Ma'am.

Mela : Take out that Alif Bachpan file, and bring it here.

Kala : Yes, Ma'am.

*(*Kala *searches among the files, takes out the relevant file and puts it on Ms. Malani's table.)*

Mela : *(Studying the file)* Hmm. Yes. This is the case *(Tosses the file to* Swasthi*)*. Here. Now study the case carefully. I want both of you to dig out all the relevant laws on the subject and prepare a written brief for me, even though I may not need it eventually.

(Just then the phone on the table rings. Ms. Malani *picks it up.)*

Mela : *(Very stern)* Yes ... speaking ... how much do I charge? Fifty thousand an appearance. No, I'm afraid I cannot reduce the rate. Now don't waste my time *(Bangs down the receiver)*. The way some people try and bargain. It's disgusting. After all they are asking for Mela Malani, not any Amar, Akbar or Anthony. *(Turns to Swasthi)* I'm, afraid I have to rush now. *(Looks at her watch)* I have a constitutional matter coming up in a few minutes in Court no. 14. Busy yourself, both of you. Kala, help him out.

(Exit Ms. Malani, *with her entourage of clerks.)*

Kala : Can you tell me why she is so pompous?

Swasthi : I don't know, but can you tell me why senior lawyers resemble each other so much.

Kala : Are seniors on your planet like this as well?

Swasthi : Oh, yes! Mine is more terrible, I think. He doesn't command a very big practice unlike Ms. Malani, and in many ways that makes it much tougher for me.

Kala : What do you mean?

Swasthi : I've noticed that Madam Mela has many clerks to assist her. I'm sure she makes you do lawyer's work, nothing else.

Kala : Why, what does your senior require you to do?

Swasthi : All his clerical work as well. It was all right in the beginning, because even that is something to be learnt, but I'm sick of it now. And to top it all he hardly pays me anything.

Kala : I somehow feel it's not so bad if he pays you less because after all as you've said he isn't making very much himself. Mela makes millions, but gives me next to nothing.

Swasthi : But you're unmarried, aren't you?

Kala : *(Coyly)* How did you guess?

Swasthi : I just had a feeling. You look so young and...fresh.

Kala : Oh, thank you, Sir, It's very sweet of you to say so. Yes, you're right, it must be more difficult for you. Your partner, I imagine, doesn't work for a living.

Swasthi : That's right.

Kala : Anyhow, why are we wasting our time talking about these creeps? As you've rightly said, they're all one and the same.

(They are both silent for a while, Swasthi *is staring at her.)*

Kala : Is there something wrong with your eyes, or are you staring at me?

Swasthi : *(Blushes)* Actually you are very beautiful, you know. I was just admiring you.

Kala : That's the second compliment you've given me in the space of two minutes. Do you really think so? *(Simpering)* Mela doesn't think so. She has never tried to take advantage of me.

Swasthi : *(In a disbelieving tone)* Never taken advantage of you! Of course she takes advantage of you. All seniors take advantage of their juniors.

Kala : I didn't mean it that way. All seniors take advantage of their juniors by paying them a pittance. I mean, otherwise.

Swasthi : *(Bewildered)* Otherwise? How do you mean?

Kala : You know what I mean.

Swasthi : *(Still confused)* Oh! I see.

Kala : *(Musing)* I suppose it's because she is happily married.

Swasthi : What does her husband do?

Kala : Husband! Never heard of such a word before. What does it mean?

Swasthi : *(Trying to explain)* The person she is married to. He would be her husband.

Kala : Are you drunk? She wouldn't be married to a he. It's against the law. She could only marry another she.

Swasthi : *(A glimmer of understanding dawning now)* Is that so? Now I understand. Is this the system followed in your planet? So who is Ms. Malani married to?

Kala : A well known female architect. They have been

married for twenty years now. Anyhow, let's not talk about her. Tell me about your plans. Where are you planning to stay while you are here?

Swasthi : *(Doubtfully)* I don't really know. I suppose I could go back to that hotel, Gaylord.

Kala : Why do you want to waste money? Gaylord will be frightfully expensive. Why don't you move in with me? You can save money and buy something for your spouse, when it's time for you to return.

Swasthi : Thank you very much. Yes, I would like to stay with you. Are you sure your landlord won't have any objections?

Kala : Of course he wouldn't mind. Why should he mind? It would be different if you were a girl, but you're only a man. Come on. Pick up your bags. Let's go.

(Exit Swasthi *and* Kala*)*

ACT TWO
Scene III

Kala's Apartment

Kala : Does your planet have a written constitution?

Swasthi : Our planet doesn't have one constitution. There would well over be a hundred constitutions. Our planet is divided into about one hundred and sixty countries and most of them have written constitutions, but different from each other.

Kala : Strange. I suppose the explanation for this is that yours is a very young planet. Even in Gayland this was the situation till the revolution took place two hundred years ago. Before that there were scores of little countries managed by barbarians, people who indulged in strange sexual practices. There was a population explosion which took place due to these barbarians. They simply didn't understand when you tried explaining to them that the population was already too much for our small planet. Each barbarian couple, which comprised a man and a woman insisted on having two or three children of their own.

Swasthi : What did the revolutionary government do?

Kala : The revolutionary government outlawed heterosexuality and marriage between opposite sexes as being immoral and a crime against society. This has resulted in enormous benefits to society.

Swasthi : Yet, tell me if sexual intercourse between a man and a women is a crime, how are children conceived?

Kala : After the technological revolution, it is no longer necessary that a woman should get pregnant or that a man should impregnate her with his sperm. All children are conceived and born in the reproduction factory.

Swasthi : Who brings up these children?

Kala : All children are brought up in institutions managed by the government. No one is permitted to know who their biological parents are. This way the child grows up free and unattached. More importantly, the population is completely regulated. It is of course permissible that a lawfully married couple can apply to the government nursery for custody of a child.

Swasthi : Oh! I see. Now what happens if a man and a woman are caught having sexual intercourse?

Kala : It's classified as a serious crime. They could go to jail for up to fourteen years. In fact the case Ms. Malani has asked us to prepare concerns one such crime. It's all the more sensational because it has been committed by two film stars, Alif Bachpan and Lekha.

Swasthi : What kind of physical intimacy between a man and a woman is against the law?

Kala : If a man and a woman have sexual intercourse, it is against the law and is regarded as a crime. But you're right.

Swasthi : So if a man and a woman are simply found kissing or holding hands, it would not be regarded as a crime.

Kala : Not under this section, it won't. You are quite a smart guy actually, you know. You have figured out the rules pretty fast.

Swasthi : If intercourse is necessary for the crime to take place, how did this particular couple get caught? Surely they must have been having it off within the privacy of their bedroom?

Kala : What actually happened was that a film journalist had come to interview Alif. According to his statement, he rang the bell twice, then realised that it was not working. He knocked on the door but there was no response. He got suspicious because he could hear some noises inside and peeped in through a window. They were at that moment both making love to each other. He was carrying his camera and managed to take a few photographs of them in flagrant delict. These were published by the film magazine. It was a major scoop for the journalist. After that of course the police had to swing into action. Both film stars have been arrested and sentenced to imprisonment by the magistrate's court. Now they have filed an appeal which is coming up before the High Court and have engaged Madam Malani to argue in their defence.

Swasthi : Let's assume for the sake of argument, Kala, that I wanted to live with a woman and share an intimate, physical relationship with her. Is there some legally permissible device by means of which I could accomplish this, or would it have to necessarily be a clandestine relationship hidden from all and conducted in secret?

Kala : *(Thinks for a while)* No, I can't think of any legal way out. Short of changing your sex, there's no way you could do that. We do permit sex change operations you know. That's perfectly legal.

Swasthi : So, if I were to change my sex and become a woman I could then legally marry you?

Kala : *(Laughs)* No, you wouldn't be able to do that. There's a contradiction in the law there. It doesn't stop you from changing your sex, but at the same time it doesn't allow you the corresponding privileges of matrimony. For example, you couldn't be registered as the official parent of a child living with you. There was this landmark case, the XYZ case.[7] A male lecturer in one of the university colleges changed his sex to become a woman so that he, or rather she could live together with a woman she was in love with. Later after a few years of living together they felt the need to have a child and applied to the government nursery for permission to have the custody of a child. X made an application to the government to be registered as an official parent of the child. X was refused permission to register as a parent on the ground that she was, legally speaking, still a man. X and his spouse Y challenged the decision of the government before the Supreme Court of Gayland, but there too, the decision went against them.

Swasthi : How terrible! Did the Supreme Court simply dismiss the case, or did they pass reasoned order?

Kala : Oh! it was a very elaborate judgement. I was reading the text only last night. *(Thinks)* Now where have I kept it *(Opens the top drawer of a chest and rummages in it for a while, finally taking out a bundle of papers)* Yes, here it is! 'The Case of X Y and Z versus Union of Gayland'. *(Turns to* Swasthi) Shall I read out the relevant extracts from it? Are you interested?

Swasthi : Yes, yes! It ties up with the Alif Bachpan case in some fashion, doesn't it?

Kala : Yes, it does. *(Flips a couple of pages)* Yes! Let me read out the facts first. *(Begins reading)* 'The first applicant X was born in 1955 and works as a lecturer. X is a male-to-female transsexual and will be referred throughout this judgement using the female pronoun. Since 1979 she has lived in a permanent and stable union with the second applicant, Y, a woman born in 1959. X was born with a male body but in 1975 she started taking hormone treatment to live and work as a woman. In 1979, she began living with Y and later that year she underwent gender reassignment surgery, having been accepted for treatment after counselling and psychological testing'.[8] Are the facts clear, Swasthi?

Swasthi : Very clear, Kala. The years you've mentioned point to the fact the X has been living happily with this woman Y for seventeen, eighteen years.

Kala : Exactly! Their problems arose only when they brought home a child. After the female child, whom we shall call Z, began living with the couple, after about a year or so, in 1990 X and Y applied to be formally registered as the parents of Z. They felt this was necessary for the purpose of school admissions, etcetera. They were interviewed by a specialist in January, 1991 and although their application was supported by two medical references, it was further referred to an Ethics Committee. (Pauses) It was however turned down.

Swasthi : And they appealed against this decision to the Court?

Kala : That's right. *(Reads aloud)* 'The applicants submitted that the lack of legal recognition of the relationship between X and Y amounted to a violation of Article 8 of the Constitution, which provides that:

1. Everyone has the right to be respected for his private and family life, his home and his correspondence.
2. There shall be no interference by a public authority on the exercise of this except as in accordance with the law and is necessary in a democratic society in the interest of national security, public safety or the economic well

> being of the planet, for the prevention of disorder or crime, for the protection of health or morals, or for the protection of the rights and freedoms of others.

The government denied that Article 8 was applicable and in the alternative, claimed that there had been no violation.'[9] Clear, so far?

Swasthi : Yes.

Kala : *(Continues to read)* 'The applicants submitted that they had shared a "family life" within the meaning of Article 8 since Z's birth. They emphasized that, according to the jurisprudence of the Courts of Gayland, social reality, rather than formal legal status was decisive. Thus, it was important to note that X had irrevocably changed many of her physical characteristics and provided financial and emotional support to Y and Z. To all appearances, the applicants lived as a traditional family'. *(Pauses)* The Court accepted the government plea that the concept of 'family life' did not apply to the relationship between X and Y or X and Z. They reasoned that X and Y had to be treated as a man and a woman living together, because X was still regarded as a male under the law and a complete change of sex was not medically possible.

Swasthi : *(Sounding depressed)* That sounds pretty final.

Kala : Tell me something, how does the situation here compare with things on your planet? Is your society better disposed towards heterosexuals?

Swasthi : Mmm.

Kala : Does that mean 'yes'?

Swasthi : *(Hesitates)* Yes.

Kala : I'm so glad heterosexuals aren't prosecuted everywhere. *(Turns thoughtful)* I wonder why people on our planet are so intolerant. *(Muses)* Could be on account of King Sol's book.

Swasthi : Is this your religious text? I must take a copy for my wife. She loves reading religious stuff.

Kala : You see Swasthi, after the revolution, King Sol wrote down all his experiences in a book. In most houses on the plant you will find a copy of it. There are a few passages in it that King Sol not only felt heterosexuality could create population problems, but he also took a very harsh view of it *per se*. During the period of the revolution there were these two cities of sin, Salami and Gumrah,[10] which were completely destroyed because they were peopled by heterosexuals.

Swasthi : But there may have been some good homosexual people living there as well.

Kala : You're absolutely right. There was one good family, Spot's family. This family was saved because King Sol intervened with God himself. *(Picks up a book from the shelf)* Here, I'll read it out. It's quite short. *(Begins reading)* 'And King Sol came near and said, "Would You also destroy the righteous with the wicked? Suppose there were fifty righteous within the city; would You also destroy the place and not spare it for the fifty righteous that were in it? Far be it from You to do such a thing as this to slay the righteous with the wicked, so that the righteous shall be as the wicked; far be it from You! Shall not the judge of all the planet do right?"

And the Lord said, "If I find in Salami fifty righteous men within the city, then I will spare all the place for their sakes."

Then King Sol answered "Indeed, now I who am but dust and ashes have taken it upon myself to speak to the Lord; Suppose there were five less than the fifty righteous; would you destroy all of the city for lack of five?"

And he said, "If I find there forty-five, I will not destroy it."

Then he spoke to him yet again and said, "Suppose there should be forty found there?"

And he said, "I will not do it for the sake of forty."

And he said, "Let not the Lord be angry and I will speak. Suppose thirty should be found there?
And he said, "I will not do it if I find thirty there."
Then he said, "Indeed now I have taken it upon myself to speak to the Lord. Suppose twenty should be found there?"
And he said, "I will not destroy it for the sake of twenty."
And he said, "Let not the Lord be angry and I will speak, but once more. Suppose ten should be found there?"
And he said, "I will not destroy it for the sake of ten."[11]

Swasthi : But the city did get destroyed in the end, didn't it? On the other hand you say there was this virtuous homosexual family.

Kala : It wasn't a very large family. There were fewer than ten members. However they were helped to escape to safety by the Lord. Here, let me read out the relevant passages. It will make things very clear. *(Begins reading)* 'Salami's depravity'.

Now the two angels came to Salami in the evening and Spot was sitting in the gate of Salami. When Spot saw them, he rose to meet them, and he bowed himself with his face towards the ground.

And he said, "Here now my Lords, please turn in to your servant's house and spend the night and wash your feet; then you may rise early and go on your way," And they said, "No, but we will spend the night in the open square."

But he insisted strongly, so they turned in to him and entered his house. Then he made them a feast, and baked unleavened bread and they ate.

Now before they lay down the men of the city, the men of Salami both old and young, all the people from every quarter, surrounded the house.

And they called to Spot and said to him, "Where are the ladies who came to you tonight? Bring them out to us, so that we may know them carnally?"

So Spot went out to them through the doorway, shut the

door behind him and said, "Please, my brethren, do not do so wickedly! See now, I have sons who have unknown a man; please let me bring them out to you, and you may do to them as you wish; only do nothing to these ladies, since this is the reason they have come under the shadow of my roof".

And they said, "Stand back!" Then they said, "This one came in to sojourn, and he keeps acting as a judge, now we will deal worse with you than with them". So they pressed hard against the man Spot and came near to break down the door. But the ladies reached out their hands and pulled Spot into the house with them and shut the door. And they struck the men who were at the doorway of the house with blindness, both small and great, so that they, became weary trying to find the door.

Then the angels said to Spot, "Have you anyone else here? son-in-law, your sons, your daughters, and whomever you have in the city, take them out of this place! For we will destroy this place, because the outcry against them has grown great before the face of the Lord, and the Lord has sent us to destroy it."[12]

(Kala *pauses here, then reads on)*

'When the morning dawned, the angels urged Spot to hurry, saying, "Arise, take your spouse and your two sons who are here, lest you be consumed in the punishment of the city."

And while he lingered the ladies took hold of his hand, his Spouse's hand, and the hands of his two sons, the Lord being merciful to him and they brought him out and set him outside the city. So it came to pass when they had brought them outside, that she said, "Escape for your life! Do not look behind you, nor stay anywhere in the plains. Escape to the mountains, lest you be destroyed."[13]

(Kala *pauses to take her breath, then continues)*

'Then the Lord rained brimstone and fire on Salami and Gumrah from the Lord out of the heavens.

So he overthrew those cities, all the plain, all the inhabitants of the cities, and what grew on the ground.

But his Spouse looked behind him and he became a pillar of salt'.[14]

Swasthi : Just for looking back! That sounds rather harsh. A pillar of salt! Quite a spot to be in. I wonder if it was consumed later.

Kala : Don't interrupt, Swasthi. Listen to these last two paragraphs. They sound quite poetic.
'And King Sol went early in the morning to the place where he had stood before the Lord. Then he looked towards Salami and Gumrah, and towards all the land of the plain; and he saw the smoke of the land which went up like the smoke of a furnace. And it came to pass when God destroyed the cities of the plain, that God remembered King Sol and sent Spot out of the midst of the overthrow, when He overthrew the cities in which Spot had dwelt.'
So now do you get the picture, Mr. Swasthi? These are the passages the heterophobic people cite when they wish to convince others that heterosexuality is an evil, which must not be condoned. It's lucky I'm not very religious, otherwise I too might have been influenced.

Swasthi : Don't you believe in God, Kala?

Kala : *(In a very sincere tone)* I do, I do! Circle my heart and hope to die!

Swasthi : So, what do you feel about these passages?

Kala : I believe that they must be seen in context, and interpreted according to the times we live in. Wouldn't you agree?

Swasthi : Yes, of course, I agree with you Kala. Yet if this is the background to Section 377, it's lucky that X and Y didn't get prosecuted like Alif and Lekha.

Kala : They couldn't very well have done that once they permitted the sex reassignment surgery. After all that too was a government decision. The operation is irreversible and X couldn't have gone back to life as a man.

Swasthi : Poor Alif and Lekha. I wonder how it must have happened that they weren't more cautious.

Kala : Oh, there is an explanation for that! It was raining that night after a storm, and they probably didn't think anyone would come to visit them. Come, let us try and reconstruct the scene of the crime. Close your eyes and listen to me.

(Swasthi *closes his eyes obediently.)*

Kala : They must have returned from shooting in the evening and Lekha must have asked, 'Alif, who were you shooting with?' and he must have replied, 'Binod Khanna'.

(A sound of a motor running comes in. Kala *is speaking and* Swasthi *is listening to her, his eyes closed.)*

ACT TWO

Scene IV

The House of filmstars Alif and Lekha

Lekha : Who were you shooting with today?

Alif : Binod Khanna. And you?

Lekha : Tridevi. It was a really hectic day. We had to do one of these new fangled dance routines so popular with the audience these days, seven times before the dance director was satisfied. It was really exhausting. Tridevi dances too well for my liking actually. It puts me in the shade. I much prefer to do these dance routines with Bahaduri or Ruhee.

Alif : You look quite tired, my dear. Can I make you some coffee?

Lekha : Yes, I would like that. I have a splitting headache.

(Alif *goes and brings some coffee for* Lekha.*)*

Lekha : *(sipping gratefully)* It's well made. Your spouse will be very happy with you.

Alif : Would you like me to press your head?

Lekha : You are a dear. No, thanks. I'm feeling better now with the coffee.

Alif : You are the one who is going to get a spouse, not me. I read somewhere that you are planning to get married to Tridevi.

Lekha : You know what these gossip magazines are like. Never believe a word they print. I do like Tridevi. She is a nice person and I probably wouldn't mind having a fling with her, but marriage? That's out of the question.

Alif : Do you know I have been approached by a film maker to do an offbeat film. It has a heterosexual theme.

Lekha : Take my advice and don't take it up. It's sure to get banned. We are living in an extremely intolerant society. Then there is that new killer disease which you can contract if you indulge in heterosexual intercourse. No, dearie, the censor board is certain to block it up for years to come.

Alif : Actually all this talk about how this new disease gets spread is completely unfounded. That disease has nothing to do with heterosexuality. These people are being targeted unnecessarily. I wonder why we are such a closed society especially since there is now no fear of over population. Why do we fear heterosexuality so much? Is it because all of us actually do have a latent heterosexual streak in us?

Lekha : Hmm. There is something in what you say. I think basically all human beings are bisexual.

Alif : *(Hesitating)* For example I have never told you ... but in fact I find you very attractive.

Lekha : *(Shocked)* Good God! And I thought that I was going mad having these crazy thoughts about you.

Alif : Really?

Lekha : Yes. Come, give me a kiss.

Alif : I don't mind if I do.

(Just then there is a rumbling and crackling sound of thunder and lightning.)

Lekha : There is a storm outside. The evening papers predicted rain. It looks like it must have started. But if you are going to kiss me, first pull those curtains completely.

Alif : Who is going to venture out in such weather? Have no fear.

*(*Alif *comes towards* Lekha *who is lying in bed and kissed her.)*

Lekha : That was nice. Do it some more.

Alif : Some more! *(Kisses her again)* Oh, you lovely girl. Why hadn't realised this about us before?

(They embrace each other. Outside, photojournalist rings the bell.)

Lekha : Did somebody ring the bell?

Alif : I didn't hear anything. Must be the wind.

(The photographer knocks on the door.)

Lekha : What was that noise? Is somebody knocking on the door?

Alif : You are imagining things, my darling. It's nobody. Nobody would come out in such a storm. It was probably just the sound of the wind you heard again. Help me unfasten this hook now.

Lekha : Kiss me again. I think I am just feeling too uptight.

(They make love. Outside, the photojournalist has by now moved to the window behind which the curtains are not fully drawn and he takes his pictures.)

ACT TWO
Scene V
Kala's Apartment

Swasthi : *(Talking to himself, his eyes closed)* Come, give me a kiss, Alif Bachpan. *(Suddenly wakes up)* Where am I?

Kala : In Gayland. Where else could you be? You poor dear! You were so tired that you fell asleep while I was telling you what must have happened on that fateful night between Alif Bachpan and Mela Malani, sorry Lekha. Gee, I guess that was a Freudian slip.

Swasthi : I don't understand why I am feeling so tired.

Kala : You must be suffering from jetlag. Travelling can be really exhausting especially between two planets. I'm glad I didn't become a travelling saleswoman. Can I get you a cup of tea? Or would you prefer some fresh orange juice?

Swasthi : Some orange juice, I think.

(Kala *goes to a section of the room where a mixer is placed and some oranges are kept and starts making some juice for* Swasthi.)

Swasthi : *(Aside)* She is really so nice, and attractive too. My wife never asks me if I would like a cup of tea even after a hard day's work.

(Kala *comes with a glass of orange juice.)*

Swasthi : *(Drinking the juice)* Now I feel much better. Tell me something, Kala, how come you haven't married?

Kala : Oh, well! I guess I've been concentrating on my career. Secondly, I just haven't come across Miss Right so far. There have been some proposals from some nice attractive women, but I don't want to get married for the sake of marriage. What do you think?

Swasthi : I think you are being very sensible.

Kala : What about your spouse? How did the two of you get married? Fell in love suddenly or was it a long affair?

Swasthi : *(Hesitantly)* We had an arranged marriage.

Kala : What on Gayland is that?

Swasthi : On my planet, in the country I live in, many marriages get arranged through relatives and friends.

Kala : Really? That's incredible! I can understand them introducing you to some suitable fellow, but marriage? It's almost like a never ending blind date.

Swasthi : It's not so bad these days. You get to meet your would be spouse a few times before you decide.

Kala : All the same it must be rather risky. What about your case? Did it work out well for you?

Swasthi : I guess so.

Kala : Do your interests match? Is she also a lawyer?

Swasthi : No, my spouse stays at home, and reads religious books.

Kala : Right. I remember now. You did tell me how expensive it was to manage your affairs. In a way it's good she is not a lawyer. The home could then turn into a courtroom with the lawyers arguing all the time, couldn't it?

Swasthi : She... I mean my spouse argues quite a lot even now.

Kala : What are your fights about? You look like a reasonable guy to me.

Swasthi : Most of the arguments concern money. My spouse is not very happy with me because I'm not earning much as a junior lawyer.

Kala : That's very reasonable on her part. In that case she should go to work. I wouldn't stand for it if my spouse made much complaints.

Swasthi : My spouse is very fond of dressing up well, and there just isn't enough money for new clothes every month.

Kala : Don't we all like to dress and eat well? I admire your loyalty to your spouse, but you're defending the indefensible, Mr Swasthi.

Swasthi : Well...thanks for seeing my point of view.

Kala : Why don't you go to sleep now? Do you need pyjamas? You can wear one of mine.

Swasthi : *(Embarrassed)* No. No, thank you. I have brought my night suit with me. (Digs out a crumpled pyjama from his suitcase) Where is the bathroom?

Kala : Silly, why are you going to the bathroom to change. It's not as if you were a woman. You are a man. You can change here itself.

Swasthi : No, I think the bathroom will be better.

Kala : All right. Suit yourself. The bathroom is right there in the corner (points at it). You are a funny fellow. I am going to change into my nightdress right here. I hope you don't have any objections to that.

(Swasthi *goes into the bathroom to change,* Kala *changes in the bedroom.* Swasthi *returns to the room, wearing his nightsuit.)*

Kala : I bought a double bed thinking that sometime I may have a guest staying overnight. As a matter of fact, you are the first guest I am having ever since I moved into this apartment. You can sleep on that bed and I will sleep on this one, since I am used to it.

Swasthi : *(Nervous)* No, no. I couldn't sleep here.

Kala : Why ever not?

Swasthi : I don't trust myself.

Kala : You don't trust yourself! You don't trust yourself, to do what?

Swasthi : *(Thinking fast)* I might mistake you for my spouse while I'm asleep.

Kala : You are getting the hang of the Gayland vocabulary at last. Even if you make such a mistake, I will understand. Don't worry.

Swasthi : *(Anxiously)* Are the curtains fully drawn?

Kala : More or less. Except for that window *(Points to a window without curtains)*. I have to buy some curtain cloth to cover that.

Swasthi : Then it is far too dangerous. I'll tell you what, I'll sleep on the carpet.

Kala : You will feel uncomfortable.

Swasthi : No, no. I'm quite used to sleeping on the carpet. Sometimes at home my wife, I mean my spouse gives me a kick, throws me off the bed. Then I sleep on the floor.

Kala : You will feel hot on the carpet. Such nice fresh linen on the bed and good mattresses too. I must say you have strange customs and practices on your planet. But if you insist, well, so be it.

ACT THREE

Scene I

The office of Ms. Mela Malani

(After three weeks Swasthi *and* Kala *are sitting quietly along with the typist and the munshi, while* Ms. Mela Malani *is pacing up and down rehearsing various arguments to be used in the case.)*

Mela : One other method is to challenge the constitutional validity of Section 377 itself. *(Turns to her junior)* Kala, take out a copy of the *Gayland Penal Code*.

Kala : Yes, Ma'am.

Mela : Have you got it?

Kala : Yes, Ma'am.

Mela : Read Section 377.

Kala : *(Starts reading)* 'Section 377. Unnatural offences — Whoever voluntarily has carnal intercourse against the order of nature with any man, woman or animal shall be punished with imprisonment of either description for a term which may extend to ten years and shall also be liable to a fine.'[15]

Mela : Is that all?

Kala : No. There is an explanation too at the end of the Section.

Mela : Read it.

Kala : 'Explanation — Penetration is sufficient to constitute the carnal intercourse necessary to the offence described in the section.'[16]

Mela : Hmm. Now what is meant by the expression 'against the order of nature.' Can anything really be against the order of nature?

Swasthi : *(Interrupting, a trifle hesitantly)* I read somewhere that 'Man is simply nature trying to understand itself'.

Mela : *(Leaps at the statement)* That's a very clever statement. What did you say? Just repeat it.

Swasthi : *(Repeats)* 'Man is simply nature trying to understand itself'.

Mela : *Munshiji,* write that down. It's a philosophical statement. Can anything ever actually be unnatural? Justice Bhagwanti will like it. It is likely that the case will come up before her. *(gives Kala a mildly threatening look)* Why didn't you think of that? All right, now take out the *Constitution of Gayland.*

Kala : Yes, Ma'am. *(Takes out a copy)*

Mela : Read Article 14. Let's see what it says.

Kala : *(Reads aloud)* 'Article 14. Equality before law — The state shall not deny to any person equality before the law or equal protection of the laws within the territory of Gayland.'[17]

Mela : *(Speaking in a declamatory style)* Now we can argue that Section 377 violates the equality clause enshrined in Article 14 of the Constitution. All persons are to be treated equally by the law. If two persons indulge in homosexual intercourse, it is not a crime. In fact, society looks upon it approvingly. Then whey should heterosexual intercourse be treated differently? In both cases there is no complainant since sexual intercourse has taken place with the consent of both the parties. Therefore, Your Ladyship, to criminalise a certain kind of sexual intercourse is unconstitutional and violative of the equality clause enshrined in Article 14 of the Constitution.

(Everybody in the office claps.)

Munshi : That was a brilliant argument, Madam!
Typist : Absolutely brilliant, Madam!
Swasthi : *(Slightly less enthusiastic)* Brilliant, Ma'am!
Kala : *(Obviously unwilling)* Brilliant.

*(*Mela Malani *gives a low bow and continues.)*

Mela : A further argument, Your Honour in support of my case. Section 377 is enshrined in Chapter 16 of the *Gayland Penal Code* which deals with offences affecting the human body and life. Now, in the case of all the offences listed under this chapter, from causing simple hurt to murder, there is an offender and separately a victim of the crime.
Kala : *(Interrupts in a triumphant tone)* What about adultery?
Mela : *(Frowns, speaks icily)* Adultery, my dear Kala, is included in the offences listed under Chapter 20 which deals with offences relating to marriage, not under this particular Chapter.
Kala : *(Sounding deflated now)* Yes, Ma'am. Sorry, Ma'am.
Mela : *(Continues)* In the case of Section 377, as I was saying Your Honour, what is extraordinary is that there is no victim of the crime. *(Repeats with emphasis)* There is no victim. *(Dramatically)* There is no dead body, but a murder has been committed. *(Softly)* No harm whatsoever has been caused to anybody. Then what business does the state have to violate the privacy of two individuals and say *(Angrily)* 'You have committed a crime.' *(Softly)* They have not harmed anyone.

(Everybody in the office claps loudly once again.)

Munshi : That was brilliant, Madam!

Typist : (making an O with his thumb and finger) Brilliant, Madam!

Swasthi : Brilliant

Kala : Ball-ant.

*(*Ms. Malani *bows, then continues.)*

Mela : *(Addressing* Swasthi *and* Kala*)* Now listen both of you. Tomorrow being Sunday it's an off day for both of you, but instead of simply wasting your time, I want you to dig out the relevant case law, put it all together and make a written brief of all the arguments for me. Kala, I want you to go through the Government reports and get me all the latest census figures because there is yet another third line of argument which I would like to advance before the Court. In earlier judgements of the Supreme Court, it has been held that Section 377 is constitutionally valid, because without it the Government may be unable to keep a check on the population growth. The Court has held that these heterosexuals produce a lot of children unmindful of the social consequences, and therefore Section 377 even though somewhat discriminatory is in the greater public interest. However my impression is that the latest census figures indicate that population levels have fallen drastically. In fact, right now workers at the reproduction factory are being asked to work overtime in order to ensure that the population level is maintained and does not slip down further.

One more thing. This is for you, Kala. I want you to go to a Medical bookstore and pick up a copy of the latest edition of a study by Dr. Alfred Kinsey on sexual behaviour. Bring this book and all relevant information with you when you come to Court on Monday.

Kala : Yes, Ma'am.

Swasthi : Yes, Ma'am. Ma'am do you think the High Court will strike down Section 377 as being unconstitutional and *ultra vires* the Constitution of Gayland?

Mela : *(Thoughtfully)* That depends actually on whose Court this matter comes up before on Monday. There are two possibilities. It could come up before either Justice Bhagwanti or Jack the Ripper. If it comes up before Justice Bhagwanti then we have a fairly good chance that the Court will hear the arguments at length and ultimately even pass judgements declaring Section 377 to be unconstitutional and *ultra vires* of the Constitution of Gayland. On the other hand if it comes up before Jack the Ripper, he won't accept the constitutional arguments. He is a puritan, a moralist who strictly believes in the religious idea that God made man in order that he cohabit with man and woman in order that she cohabit with woman. He regards heterosexuality as a dangerous deviation, as immoral and evil. He is dead set against all modern progressive trends which favour a more liberal approach to the whole question of sexuality. Personally, I tend to agree with him, but a case is a case. I can argue equally well on both sides.

Swasthi : This means that if we are to win this case it must come up before Justice Bhagwanti.

Mela : *(Mysteriously)* Not necessarily. Of course since Justice Bhagwanti sits in the morning and Justice Jack in the afternoon session, we will try to manoeuvre things in such a manner that our case gets listed first thing in the morning.

Kala : Ma'am, I believe that if Justice Bhagwanti hears the case she may like to hear some case law from Uroland.

Mela : Of course! It completely slipped my mind. That's essential!

Kala : Ma'am, we haven't received their law reports for the last six months.

Mela : Hmm. Doesn't matter. Kala, would you please dig out the e-mail address of *Unirights*, a human rights organization based in Uroland?

(Kala *picks up a directory and searches for the address.)*

Mela : Have you got it?

Kala : Yes, Ma'am, I have.
(Reads aloud) unirights@spacemail.com

Mela : Okay, now before you leave the office today, I want you to send them an e-mail, explaining everything about this case and requesting them to immediately send us the copies of all the latest judgements which could possibly have a bearing on our case. Will you remember to do that?

Kala : Yes, ma'am.

Mela : And bring them with you to Court after having prepared a short note on each important case. It's very important. Justice Bhagwanti is likely to hear arguments on Monday and she loves to hear cases from their jurisdiction. She cites them now and then in her own judgements as well. I believe she's due for retirement next year, and she's very anxious to be widely recognized as an inter-planetary jurist of note before that happens. It will mean of course that she will get invited regularly to attend and speak at all those interplanetary conferences on human rights.

Kala : I'll send this e-mail immediately, Ma'am. Mr. Swasthi is there to help me.

Mela : Thank you Kala. Thank you Swasthi. Now I must go. Vista TV have called me for a television debate this evening and I must go home and change. *(Pauses)* And Kala?

Kala : Yes, Ma'am.

Mela : Do remember to ask *Unirights* to have all the

transcripts of any judgement they e-mail duly attested and certified to be true copies by the Cyber Notary Public. I don't want the High Court registry or the State Public Prosecutor to start raising technical objections of any kind.

Kala : Yes, Ma'am.

Mela : Mr. Swasthi, why are you looking so serious. Is something the matter?

Swasthi : I was just imagining the plight of Mr. Bachpan and Miss Lekha. They must be going through hell, and for something that ought to concern no one else. I do hope it is Justice Bhagwanti who hears the case on Monday morning.

Mela : Don't be so worried, Mr. Swasthi. Even if it is Jack, I will think of something. They don't call me Mela Malani, the legal eagle for nothing! All right then, I must go. See you both Monday morning nine o'clock sharp at the High Court. Okay?

Kala : Yes, Ma'am.

Swasthi : Yes, Ma'am.

(Exit Mela Malani *with* Munshi *and* typist *in tow.)*

Kala : A one-eyed crow would better describe her, don't you think? I was thinking that tomorrow being Sunday, I would get up late, clean up the apartment and then go out and sit in a park. Now this bitch has spoilt everything by giving both of us work to do.

Swasthi : Maybe we can go and sit in a park and work there itself. That won't be so depressing. After we have finished our work, we can just laze about in the sun.

Kala : *(Consoled)* Yes, maybe we can do that. Let me just send off that e-mail to *Unirights* now and we can leave as soon as they have sent the judgements.

ACT THREE
Scene II
A park

(Sunday.)

Swasthi : She had said that I should wait for her under this *peepul* tree, while she went and brought the book from the medical bookstore. It is the only thing that remains to be done, otherwise we have more or less finished our preparation for the case coming up tomorrow before the Hon'ble High Court of Gayland. I hear footsteps. Somebody is approaching. Perhaps it is she.

Enter Phulwa *and* Geeta, *the lesbian couple.*

Geeta : This looks like a nice, quiet place.

Phulwa : Yes, it does.

Geeta : There is nobody here except for that creep sitting by himself over there.

Phulwa : Yes. We must come here more often. It's much better than all those stuffy cinema halls. Let's sit down on the grass, shall we?

(They sit down.)

Geeta : How long will we keep on meeting like this?

Phulwa : You are under-age right now, my darling. Do you know that technically you are incapable of giving consent and that I could be charged with raping a minor for making love to you.

Geeta : I am going to be eighteen next month.

Phulwa : As soon as we celebrate your eighteenth birthday, my darling we shall go and get our marriage license.

Geeta : It's only a month away, but it seems like a year.

Phulwa : *(Sympathetically)* I know.

Geeta : Come kiss me.

Swasthi : *(Talking to himself)* I wonder what that young girl sees in an old hag like her. Love, ways are truly strange. I hear footsteps. Perhaps it is Kala.

Enter Balam *and* Navneet, *a homosexual couple. They walk around and then finally sit down on a bench inside the park.*

Balam : I told you this place is really cool and quiet. It's practically deserted except for that couple sitting over there and that freak sitting under the *peepul* tree.

Navneet : How come you know of all these places? You never came here with me before. Who have you brought here, tell me?

Balam : Listen, I tell you. You are a really suspicious guy.

Navneet : I think I have good reason to feel that way.

Balam : What good reason do you have?

Navneet : I saw you drinking coffee with that fellow Shanney the other day inside Gaylord restaurant.

Balam : All right. So I was having coffee with him. What's wrong with that? Can't a guy even have coffee with another fellow?

Navneet : I don't like that Shanney fellow.

Balam : That's okay by me. I didn't like him particularly myself, but a guy's got to be civil. He asked me if I would share a pot of coffee with him, and it would have looked too rude to refuse, so I accepted.

Navneet : I think he is trying to make a play for you.

Balam : Make a play for me? Of course not. You are being ridiculous. Come on, Navneet, you see me having coffee with a guy and you think he's making a play for me.

Navneet : That's not the only place I remember seeing you both in.

Balam : What do you mean? I haven't met him anywhere else.

Navneet : *(In a quiet tone)* Are you very sure of this, Balam?

Balam : Yes, of course.

Navneet : Don't lie to me, Balam. The day before yesterday, around the time of the matinee show, I saw both of you standing together outside the Gaiety Multiplex.

Balam : *(Rattled)* If you saw both of us together, how come you didn't come forward to say hello. What were you doing there? Spying on us? You knew very well I was going to see *Playing Ball*, at the Gaiety and I had even asked you to come with me for the matinee show, but no, Your Lordship had to go for some job interview in the afternoon. It appears to me, Navneet, that you're the one who is being deceitful.

Navneet : You can't accuse me of deceit, Balam. You know perfectly well that I never lie to you. I was going to attend the job interview in one of the red double decker buses and from window seat, as the bus passed the Gaiety theatre crossing, I saw both of you standing outside the cinema hall. I had half a mind to get off the bus, but I couldn't for I had this interview, as I have already told you.

Balam : All right. That explains it.

Navneet : Satisfied?

Balam : Yes. But listen Navneet, if I can accept your explanations so easily, why are you so suspicious? I had gone for the movie, as you know already, and over there outside the cinema hall I accidentally bumped into Shanney, so we got chatting. What's the big deal about that?

Navneet : *(With sweet sarcasm)* And then I suppose you decide to see the movie together.

Balam : As it happened we had both come alone, so that was only natural, wasn't it?

Navneet : And was it also natural for you not to tell me anything about this meeting?

Balam : It was a harmless, innocent encounter with Shanney. Besides I didn't think you'd be interested.

Navneet : And when two hours ago, I asked you very casually whether you'd met him recently, you said, no, you hadn't.

Balam : I'd forgotten!

Navneet : *(Raises his eyebrows suspiciously)* Forgotten? Forgotten that you'd met him the day before yesterday.

Balam : Well, it was actually because... because I know you've got this terrible, suspicious mind.

Navneet : And you thought I might put two and two together?

Balam : And make twenty two! Yes, I thought that.

Navneet : Did you really think that, Balam? I hope you are not two timing me.

Balam : Come on, Navneet. Stop behaving like this. As a matter of fact, Shanney is one person you should never even dream of suspecting.

Navneet : So there are others?

Balam : I didn't say that. You're just putting words into my mouth. All I'm saying is that you simply cannot link Shanney with me.

Navneet : Why can't I?

Balam : Because...because... do you know something? *(Pauses)* He is a hetero!

Navneet : *(Shocked)* Hetero? Shanney? I don't believe you.

Balam : All right. Don't. I'll prove it to you. Tomorrow morning we'll go together to the book seller at Seagull Building who sells literature on alternative lifestyles. I will buy and present you with a copy of *Musings* a just-released collection of hetero poetry, written by Shanney and published by the Hetero Men and Women Press.

Navneet : *(Suddenly in doubt)* Are you telling the truth, Balam?

Balam : Circle my heart and hope to die. Of course I am, Navneet, you suspicious guy. Why can't you believe me? If you like I'll get Shanney to personally autograph the copy for you. Will that satisfy you?

Navneet : Oh, well, I'm sorry!

Balam : As far as I am concerned, there is only one man in my life... and that's you, Navneet.

Navneet : You really mean it?

Balam : Of course! Now stop acting so insecure and give me a kiss.

Swasthi : *(Aside)* My God, these couples are really making me feel so jealous and out of place sitting alone in this park. Kala is such an attractive girl, much nicer than my wife, but if I tried to hug her or hold her hand, do you think she would mind? But wait! I hear footsteps. Surely now it must be her.

(Enter Kala *carrying a book in her hands.)*

Kala : Hi there! Sorry to have kept you waiting so long. The first medical book shop I went to didn't have a copy of the Kinsey Report, the second one had an old edition and to reach the third one I had to walk another couple of blocks.

Swasthi : Did you manage to get it finally?

Kala : Yes, what did you think I have in my hands? What have you been doing in my absence? How have you kept yourself busy?

Swasthi : I went over the case law we have unearthed. It's quite clearly mentioned in Kharak Singh's case decided by the Supreme Court of Gayland[18] that the right to privacy can be read into the right to life and liberty. That's Article 21 of the Constitution of course. I think it can be reasonably argued that Section 377 infringes the fundamental right to privacy of an individual and can be declared unconstitutional for this reason also.

Kala : Okay, let's have a quick look at all the arguments we've got. We've finished preparing a short note on each one, haven't we?

Swasthi : Yes, we have.

Kala : Will you read out the notes on arguments one by one for my benefit and then I can do the same with regard to the notes on case law from the Courts of Uroland.

Swasthi : Yes, let's do that, but first please explain to me what and where is this Uroland, and why do we keep referring to their decisions.

Kala : Uroland is the nearest planet to Gayland. Both planets have long established trade and cultural ties with each other.

Swasthi : Oh, I remember now!

Kala : What do you remember?

Swasthi : You know the escort who brought me here said that sometimes it becomes difficult to decide which planet is Gayland and which is Uroland because both are pink in colour.

Kala : Yes, but ours is much bigger. Anyhow, what I was telling you was that both our civilizations have some common features to them. We in Gayland have a stronger, more vibrant culture, but in some respects the people of Uroland are rather more progressive than we are. Our planets are in close touch with each other by means of e-mail and as far as our legal systems are concerned we frequently refer to the judgements of each others' Supreme Courts while deciding ticklish questions of law for which there are few, if any precedents.

Swasthi : I understand everything now. Shall we proceed then?

Kala : Yes, you can begin with arguments unconnected to case law.

Swasthi : All right. *(Begins reading from a piece of paper)* 'Because drafted in 1833, the Gayland Penal Code is in many respects archaic and absurd. In 1957, the Gayland Committee on heterosexual offences and prostitution under the chairmanship of Sir John Foxedon made a recommendation that adult consensual heterosexual acts be criminalised. Such a change had been recommended by Havekey Willis, eminent Gayland sexologist and author of the path breaking series on the psychology of sex. Since 1958, the Heterosexual Law Reforms Society of Gayland has campaigned for such a step.'[19]

Kala : I think that argument has been phrased quite well. The judges should be impressed by these reports. What's next?

Swasthi : The second argument concerns some reports from Uroland. *(Reads)* 'Because according to established medical opinion in Uroland, such as that of the Uroland Psychiatry Association, heterosexuality is perfectly normal, reflecting simply a different sexual orientation and pattern of loving and cannot be considered as abnormal anymore. A statement by the Association to the effect is annexed herewith. A statement made by the President, Gayland Medical Association, concurring with the Uroland Medical Association is also annexed herewith.'[20] *(Pauses)* Then we have something on human rights abuses from Uroland. *(Reads)* 'Because after years of lobbying and negotiation by Uroland heterosexual rights organizations, even a respected human rights organization such as Global Watchdog[21] has in recent years taken a stand on heterosexuality. The main report of its research project 'Global Watchdog and Heterosexuality' released in April, 1987 summarized Watchdog's exhaustive research into the persecution of heterosexual people all over the world, but concentrates mainly on the persecution of heterosexual persons. The main conclusion of the report needs to be noted and adopted by the Gayland government and civil rights organizations.'

Kala : Great! Now we have clearly outlined for the Court's benefit the fact that we have the backing of responsible and respectable medical and other professional bodies. What about the arguments relating to legal provisions?

Swasthi : I'm coming to those. We've made a note here that Section 377 is violative of Article 14 of the Constitution of Gayland since it discriminates against people on the basis of their sexual orientation. *(Reads)* 'The idea that sexual relations must take place only within a prescribed sexual format shows bias, prejudice, ignorance and lack of tolerance.'[22] *(Pauses)* This one concerns one of the global conventions. *(Reads)* 'Because the right to privacy has also been recognized by the various global conventions on human rights. Article 12 of the Universal Declaration of Human Rights states : No one shall be subjected to arbitrary interference with his privacy, family, home or correspondence, nor to attacks upon his honour or reputation.'[23] *(Flips through some pages)* Yes, here it is. We have a very clever legal argument on the actual phrasing of Section 377. *(Reads)* 'Because the expression "carnal intercourse" used in Section 377 is extremely vague and ambiguous, lending itself to diverse interpretations and for this reason also the section ought to be struck down as unconstitutional. It is pertinent to mention here that this particular section was introduced in a rushed manner by the Law Commission in 1937, with practically no debate on the issue, all because of the background under which the great revolution took place under the leadership of King Sol.'[24] Next we have, 'Because the teachings of King Sol have to be interpreted in the light of modern scientific findings,' and again, 'Because population pressures on our planet have long ceased and as such no remaining public purpose or good will be served by retaining the archaic provisions of Section 377.'

Kala : Let's look up Dr. Kinsey's report now, shall we?

Swasthi : Sure.

Kala : *(Flipping through the book for several minutes)* Here. I think I have found it. They conducted a study to determine the percentage of heterosexuals in the population. In a nutshell what he has found after examining several thousand sexual histories is that four per cent of men and two per cent of women are exclusively heterosexual and that six per cent of men are heterosexual for a significant part of their adolescence.[25]

Swasthi : I guess it's your turn now to read out the extracts from the Courts at Uroland. You were reading the judgements till late last night after we returned from office, weren't you?

Kala : Yes. I prepared some rough notes, so you'll get an idea when I read them out. You know Uroland is a federation of five states — Northern Uroland, Southern Uroland, Eastern Uroland, Western Uroland and Central Uroland — and there is as yet no verdict from their Supreme Court, but there are three important cases from the High Courts.

Swasthi : I'm listening.

Kala : *(Picks up a file and flips through it)* This one here is known as the *Boris Case,*[26] which is from Northern Uroland. The facts in the second one known as the *Dungeon Case*[27] are basically similar, and since this one came later, I'll just discuss this one, and save us some time, shall I? The facts of this case are quite simple really. Our friend Boris was a member of one of the State Parliaments. He was a self-proclaimed heterosexual and the Chairman of the Heterosexual Rights Movements in his State. He filed proceedings in one of the High Courts seeking a declaration to the effect that certain laws prohibiting heterosexual relations were invalid under the State Constitution.[28]

Swasthi : Something like Section 377 of the Gayland Penal Code.

Kala : Exactly. There were two laws he attacked. Section 62 of the Person Act, 1861 which provided that *(Reads)* 'whosoever shall attempt to commit the said abominable crime of heterosexual intercourse or shall be guilty of intimate sexual contact with a person of the opposite sex shall be guilty of misdemeanour and shall be subjected to a prison sentence not exceeding ten years.' There was also Section 11 of the Criminal Law Amendment Act, 1885 which was to the effect that *(Reads aloud)* 'any person, who, in public or in private commits... any act of gross indecency with a person of the opposite sex is guilty of misdemeanour and subject to imprisonment not exceeding two years.'

Swasthi : What does 'gross indecency' mean?

Kala : The term 'gross indecency' was not statutorily defined and was to be given meaning by Courts on the particular facts of each case.

Swasthi : Was Boris caught in the act with a woman, like in our case?

Kala : No, the facts are quite different here. Boris was actually never charged with any offence in relation to his admitted heterosexual activities.

Swasthi : Then?

Kala : He was at risk, you see. He was continuously at risk of being prosecuted on the basis of an indictment laid by the Director of Public Prosecutions.

Swasthi : In that case the Court could have simply summoned the Director and asked him of his intentions.

Kala : They did do that, but you know how lawyers are. You just can't pin them down. I'll read out what he said, *(Reads from the file)* 'In connection with this case the Director made a statement which was to the effect that the Director had no stated prosecution policy on any branch of the criminal law.[29] *(Laughs)* 'At the same time he has no unstated policy not to enforce any offence.'

Swasthi : In my country on my planet a petitioner must be able to claim to be actually affected in some way, in order to be able to challenge the constitutionality of a provision. A law cannot be challenged in the abstract.

Kala : Same was the case here. *(Reads)* 'Article 25 requires that an individual applicant should be able to claim to be actually affected by the measure of which he complains. Article 25 may not be used to fund an action in the nature of an *actio popularis* nor may it form the basis of a claim made *in abstracto* that a law contravenes the Convention.'[30] But Boris was clever. His counsel argues that the legislation had interfered with his right to respect for his private life. Boris led evidence to show that he became deeply depressed when he realized that *(Reads)* 'any overt expression of his sexuality would expose him to criminal prosecution.' He became extremely fearful of prosecution for himself as well as for the woman he had a physical relationship with.

Swasthi : That was a clever argument. *(Pauses)* So what did the Court decide?

Kala : I'll read you extracts from the judgement itself. Shall I stand and read out? It'll give me practice in case Mela falls ills or something and I have to argue instead.

Swasthi : Yes, do that.

Kala : *(Stands up, and begins speaking as if addressing a Court of Law)* Para 32 of the Boris judgement, Milord. 'In the Court's view, Mr. Boris is in substantially the same position as the applicant in the *Dungeon Case* which concerned identical legislation then in force in Northern Uroland. As was held in that case, 'either he respects the law and refrains from engaging even in private and with consenting female partners — in prohibited sexual acts in which he is disposed by reason of his heterosexual tendencies, or he commits such acts and thereby becomes liable to criminal prosecution.'[31] *(Pauses)* Your Lordship may now read Para 38 of this decision. *(Reads)* 'The Court agrees with the Commission that, with regard to the interference with an Article 8 right, the present case is indistinguishable from the *Dungeon Case*... Enforcement of legislation is a matter for the Director of Public Prosecutions who may not fetter his discretion with regard to each individual case by making a general statement of his policy in advance... as was held in that case, 'the maintenance in force of the impugned legislation constitutes a continuing interference with the applicant's right to respect for his private life... within the meaning of Article 1. In the personal circumstances of the applicant the very existence of this legislation continuously and directly affects his private life...'[32] *(Breaks off)* Are you following me, Swasthi? Right... *(Continues)* then Your Lordship may have a look at Para 42 of the judgement. *(Reads aloud)* 'It was not contended before the Commission that there is a large body of opinion in Uroland which is hostile or intolerant towards heterosexual acts committed in private between consenting adults. Nor was it argued that Uroland society had a special need to be protected from such activity. In these circumstances, the Commission concluded that the restriction imposed on the applicant under Uroland Law, by reason of its breadth and absolute character, is disproportionate to the aims sought to be achieved and therefore is not necessary for one of the reasons laid down in Article 8(2) of the Convention.'[33] *(Breaks off)* Have you got that, Swasthi?

Swasthi : Yes, I have. Oh, Kala, you're looking lovely in your pink blouse and green skirt.

Kala : Later, Swasthi, later. *(Resumes her Court manner)* Your Lordship may note that in *Boris Case* the Hon'ble High Court of Northern Uroland has approved of the earlier decision by the High Court of Southern Uroland in the *Dungeon Case* and has quoted with approval from its text. In that earlier decision the Court had enunciated the very important doctrine of margin of appreciation. I'll beg your leave to briefly read from Para 46 of the judgement in *Boris*, which refers to the earlier decision. *(Reads)* 'As in the *Dungeon Case,* "Not only the nature of the aim of the restriction but also the nature of the activities involved will affect the scope of the margin of appreciation. The present case concerns a most intimate aspect of private life. Accordingly there must exist particularly serious reasons before interferences on the part of public authorities can be legitimate for the purposes of Para 2 of Article 8. Yet the Government has adduced no evidence which would point to the existence of factors justifying the retention of the impugned laws which are additional to or of greater weight than those present in the aforementioned *Dungeon Case*." At Para 60 of its judgement of October 22, 1981, the Court noted that, "As compared with the era when the legislation was enacted, there is now a better understanding and in consequence an increased tolerance of heterosexual behaviour to the extent that in the great majority of the member states of Uroland, it is no longer considered to be necessary or appropriate to treat heterosexual practices of the kind now in question as in themselves a matter to which the sanctions of the criminal law should be applied; the Court cannot overlook the marked changes which have occurred in this regard in the domestic law of the member States." It was clear that "the authorities had refrained in recent years from enforcing the law in respect of private heterosexual acts between a consenting adult male and female capable of valid consent." There was no evidence to show that this "had been injurious to moral standards in Northern Uroland or that there had been any public demand for stricter enforcement of the law."[34] *(Breaks off)* Swasthi! Have you fallen asleep?

Swasthi : No, no, I'd just closed my eyes to hear you better. You were arguing that there is no public interest which justifies having a law.

Kala : Exactly. And even if for the sake of argument, one concedes that there may be one, it is not proportionate.

Swasthi : What does that mean?

Kala : Here, I'll read it out for you. *(Reads)* 'On the specific issue of proportionality the Court is of the opinion that such justifications as they are for retaining the law in force unamended are outweighed by the detrimental effects which the very existence of the legislative provisions in question can have on the life of a person of heterosexual orientation like the applicant.'[35] *(Reads slowly, and with emphasis)* 'Although members of the public who regard heterosexuality as immoral may be shocked, offended or disgusted by the commission by others of private heterosexual acts, this cannot on its own warrant the application of penal sanctions when it is consenting adults alone who are involved.'[36] Clear?

Swasthi : Yes, that's clear enough. Are we through now?

Kala : There's still one judgement from the High Court of Western Uroland left. *Showers versus Sadsack*[37]. This judgement undoubtedly goes against us because the High Court of Western Uroland by a 5-4 vote held that the statute criminalising heterosexual intercourse was constitutional.

Swasthi : If it goes against us, why should we cite it?

Kala : We probably won't use it, but it's best to be well prepared. The Alif and Lekha case involves the prestige of the Gayland government, and they will hire the best talent may be even appoint a special prosecutor. Just suppose they do this and the prosecution manages to get hold of a copy of *Showers versus Sadsack*. We'll look pretty silly if the Court thinks we aren't familiar with the decision.

Swasthi : That's true. If they do cite this case as a precedent, we can always take the line that this is only one case, whereas there are two High Court decisions which support our case. *Boris* and *Dungeon*. Moreover in this one case which goes against us, the majority decision prevailed by only a single vote.

Kala : Exactly.

Swasthi : What are the facts of this case?

Kala : A bit similar to ours. Sadsack was arrested in his home bedroom immediately after engaging in intercourse with a consenting female.

Swasthi : How did the cops come to know? What was the proof?

Kala : Oh! this fellow Sadsack was already under surveillance by the police, so it was easy for them to nab him and prove the facts. He was tried with the crime of heterosexual intercourse and before being tried challenged the statute.

Swasthi : Wasn't the High Court swayed by the decisions in *Boris* and *Dungeon*?

Kala : No, Uroland is a federation. The High Court of Western Uroland is not bound by those decisions, since those are judgments by Courts of equal rank. Justice White who led the majority opinion didn't accept the judgments as being applicable. I'll just read out a couple of paragraphs from Justice White's judgement and a couple from Justice Burger who supported him and you'll get an idea of the legal arguments in this case. Okay?

Swasthi : *(A bit wearily)* Go ahead.

Kala : *(Reads)* 'The issue presented is whether the Federal Constitution confers a fundamental right upon heterosexuals to engage in heterosexual intercourse and invalidates the laws of the States that still make such conduct illegal...'[38]

Swasthi : *(Thoughtfully)* A fundamental right to engage in heterosexual intercourse. That sounds rather different from saying that it's nobody's business what you do in the privacy of your bedroom with a person of the opposite sex.

Kala : Exactly. This is populist language, isn't it? This was pointed out to the judge, but he stuck to his guns. Here, this is what he said. *(Reads)* 'Even if the conduct at issue here is not a fundamental right, respondent asserts that there must be a rational basis for the law and that there is none in this case other than the presumed belief of a majority of the electorate in that heterosexual intercourse is immoral and unacceptable. This is said to be an inadequate rationale to support the law. The law, however, is constantly based on notions of morality, and if all laws representing essentially moral choices are to be invalidated under the Due Process Clause, the courts will be very busy indeed...'[39] *(Pauses)* Justice Burger, who supported Justice White wrote this with regard to the fundamental right position. *(Reads)* 'Decisions of individuals relating to heterosexual conduct have been subject to state intervention throughout the history of our civilization. Condemnation of those practices is firmly rooted in moral and ethical standards... To hold that the act of heterosexual intercourse is somehow protected as a fundamental right would be to cast aside millennia of moral teaching.'[40]

Swasthi : Let's hear what the dissenting judges had to say. That's more important from our point of view.

Kala : Okay. Justice Black who led the dissent gave a brilliant decision. Let me read you a couple of extracts from his judgement. *(Reads)* 'This case is not about "a fundamental right to engage in heterosexual intercourse" as the Court purports to declare... Rather, this case is about "the most comprehensive of rights and the right most valued by civilized men" namely, "the right to be let alone."[41]

I believe we must analyse respondent Sadsack's claim in the light of the values that underlie the constitutional right to privacy. If that right means anything, it means that, before Western Uroland can prosecute its citizens for making choices about the most intimate aspects of their lives, it must do more than assert that the choice they have made is an 'abominable crime not fit to be named among Uroland people.'[42] *(Pauses, then reads again)* 'Only the most wilful blindness could obscure the fact that sexual intimacy is a "sensitive, key relationship of human existence, central to family life, community welfare, and the development of human personality." The fact that individuals define themselves in a significant way through their intimate sexual relationships with others suggest, in a nation as diverse as ours, that there may be many "right" ways of conducting those relationships, and that much of the richness of a relationship will come from the freedom an individual has, to choose the form and nature of these intensely personal bonds.'[43] *(Pauses)* Last two paragraphs, Swasthi. *(Reads)* 'The State and the Court fail to see the difference between laws that protect public sensibilities and those that enforce private morality. Statutes banning public sexual activity are entirely consistent with protecting the individual's liberty and interest in decisions concerning sexual relations: the same recognition that those decisions are intensely private which justifies protecting them from governmental interference can justify protecting individuals from unwilling exposure to the sexual activities of others. But the mere fact that intimate behaviour may be punished when it takes place in public, cannot dictate how States can regulate intimate behaviour that occurs in intimate places...'[44] *(Pauses, then reads)* 'This case involves no real interference with the rights of others, for the mere knowledge that other individuals do not adhere to one's value system cannot be a legal cognizable interest, let alone an interest that can justify, invading the houses, hearts and minds of citizens who choose to live their lives differently.'[45] That's it, my dear!

Swasthi : Now that this last bit is over, we can just relax.

Kala : Yes. Enjoy the sun while it's there.

Swasthi : You know you are looking really beautiful in these jeans today.

Kala : You are a dear. You always say such nice things. I wish you were a girl.

Swasthi : Tell me something. What do you really think of heterosexuality?

Kala : What do I really think about it? What do you mean?

Swasthi : You know that Ms. Malani will be arguing before the High Court tomorrow that Section 377 should be scrapped, yet privately, as she confessed yesterday, she is anti-heterosexual.

Kala : She is a horrible woman. She just pretends to be liberal so that the newspapers will project her as a champion of minority rights. Basically she is a conservative and a hardcore materialist.

Swasthi : What do you think?

Kala : I think there is nothing wrong with heterosexuality so long as it is consensual. Rape is rape whether it is heterosexual rape or homosexual rape and consent is consent, whether it be for heterosexual intercourse or homosexual. Don't you agree?

Swasthi : *(Fervently)* Yes, I do. *(After a while)* Can you show me your hand?

Kala : *(Proffering it)* Here. Do you know something of palmistry?

Swasthi : No, but do you mind if I hold it for some time?

Kala : No, of course not, silly. Here, Hold it as long as you like. *(They hold hands. Swasthi moves closer. Meanwhile the other two couples are busy smooching each other.)*

(Enter Vivek, *a constable. He has been hiding behind the bushes all the while, from where he suddenly emerges.)*

Vivek : Ho! What is this I see here? *(Catches* Swasthi *by the hair)* What are you doing mister?

Swasthi : Nothing, I'm doing nothing, officer.

Vivek : I was watching you. Sitting close and holding hands. Isn't that doing something? Or were you planning

		to do something more? Come with me to the police station.
Kala	:	Listen, you are making a mistake, constable. We were only discussing a case.
Vivek	:	Tell that story to your grandmother. *(In a sneering tone)* You were discussing a case. Hah!
Kala	:	*(Angrily)* Yes. Come on. Let's go to the police station. We will see what they can do.
Swasthi	:	Wait. But officer, why are arresting only the two of us? What about those two couples?
Vivek	:	I'll let them be for today. At least what they are doing is normal. That's still okay. But the two of you? Shameless! You are the people who need to be locked up because you are responsible for drugs, for corrupting the morals of the young and for that killer disease. Now, not another word from either of you. You can say your piece before the Station House Officer.

(Exit Kala *and* Swasthi *with* Constable Vivek *leading the way.)*

ACT THREE
Scene III

Police Station

(Inside the police station, Vivek *the constable produces* Swasthi *and* Kala *before* Virender, *the Station House Officer.)*

Vivek	:	This couple here were found messing around in the public park, Sir.
Swasthi	:	Kindly clarify what 'messing around' means, constable. It is true that we were holding hands if you mean that. Anything wrong with that?
Vivek	:	There's plenty wrong with that.
Swasthi	:	What's wrong?
Viren	:	*(Intervening)* Listen mister, just keep quiet and let me first hear what the constable has to say and

then you will have an opportunity to say what you like. Yes, Constable, Go ahead.

Vivek : Yes, Sir. It happened like this. I happened to be present in the park today. At precisely 5.35 p.m. I saw this couple here holding hands and sitting so close she was practically on his lap and he was bending his head as if any moment he was going to smack her.

Swasthi : Please clarify what you mean by 'smack'.

Viren : I told you, keep quiet.

Vivek : I mean of course that he was going to kiss her and then of course they would have gone on to the heavy duty stuff, so before they could corrupt the public morals further I brought them here.

Viren : Well done, Constable. *(Turns to* Swasthi *and* Kala*)* I will have to put both of you in lockup unless...*(Pauses)*

Kala : Are you perhaps soliciting a bribe, Officer?

Viren : I was going to say 'unless your employer comes to the station to bail both of you out'. So cut the fancy talk, lady. Constable, put them both in the lockup.

Vivek : Yes, Sir.

Swasthi : You can't put me in jail. I am a visitor from outer space, a representative of another planet, and I have diplomatic immunity from being charged with any crime. And can you tell us what is the offence we have committed? We have a right to know.

Viren : Don't tell me your rights. I know all about that. You are going to be charged under Section 377 of the Gayland Penal Code. Both of you are going to be in the cooker for a long, long time. It's a very serious offence. Only the other day we had two filmstars Alif Bachpan and Lekha in the lockup charged with the same crime. Yes, filmstars! The law is the same for everybody in Gayland, be they high or low.

Swasthi : Perhaps in our case, Officer, the offence cannot be categorised under Section 377.

Viren : What do you mean?

Swasthi : Have you read Section 377 properly, Officer?

Viren : Of course, I have.

Swasthi : No, you haven't otherwise you would know that the necessary ingredients of the offence under Section 377 are absent in this case.

Viren : Of course the necessary whatever are present. Constable, get me a copy of the Penal Code.

Kala : *(Handing him their copy)* Here is copy of the Code. You can look for the Section inside.

Viren : Where did you get this from? Constable, is our copy missing?

Swasthi : *(With dignity)* It's our business to keep abreast of the law, Officer. We are lawyers. My colleague here is associated with the famous criminal lawyer, Mela Malani.

Viren : Mela Malani! My God! Both of you are working with her. Really? You must be right then. I don't have to read the Section. You tell me. What does it say?

Swasthi : It uses the word 'intercourse' officer. It says that an offence shall be made out if carnal intercourse has taken place. The explanation to the Section clarifies that penetration shall be sufficient to constitute intercourse. Now, holding hands cannot, by any stretch of imagination be said to constitute an act of carnal intercourse, can it Officer?

Viren : Yes, of course. Now I remember, In Alif Bachpan and Lekha's case there was clear proof of carnal intercourse. I'm sorry, Sir. I'm sorry, Madam. This fool of a constable disturbed your preparation for tomorrow's case. Please don't mention this incident to anyone *(Yells)* Constable!

Swasthi : Well, this time we will let you off easily. However don't make the same mistake again with anyone else, otherwise my colleague and I will see to it that you lose all those pretty badges on your shirt. You might even lose your job. Understood?

Viren : Understood, Sir. Understood, Ma'am. Very sorry indeed. *(Yells)* Constable!

Vivek : Yes, Sir.

Viren : You bloody fool. Come here at once.

Vivek : Yes, Sir.

Viren : You son of a gun. Can't you recognise decent people when you see them? Are you off your head that you have arrested these nice, decent lawyers? Go after some serious crime next time. Don't trouble innocent people sitting in parks doing their studies, preparing cases.

Vivek : Yes, Sir.

Viren : Bring out the jeep and drop this gentleman and lady to their residence or wherever they like. They have to prepare an important case.

Swasthi : *(Disdainfully)* No, I am afraid we would rather walk, wouldn't we, Kala? We wouldn't like to misuse a government vehicle, and I hope you don't either, Officer.

Viren : Yes, Sir. No, Sir.

(Exit Swasthi *and* Kala.*)*

(Outside the police station)

Kala : You were magnificent.

Swasthi : Was I?

Kala : Yes, you were. I have never seen you like this before. I wish you were a citizen of Gayland. We could have had a legal partnership and argued the pants off Mela Malani.

(Exit Swasthi *and* Kala.*)*

ACT THREE
Scene IV

A Courtroom inside the High Court of Gayland

(The stage is divided into two sections. There is one half which consists of the courtroom and the other half is a street just outside the courtroom. As the scene opens, it is early morning, the judge has yet to arrive and already there is a demonstration outside the courtroom by heterosexual activists, a sprinkling of democratic rights activists, and fans of the two filmstars who are carrying placards and banners on which are written variously, 'Release Alif and Lekha', 'Repeal Section 377', 'Stop Discrimination Against Heterosexuals', 'Admit Heterosexuals into the Army'. Geeta too can be seen among the demonstrators with her persuaded lover, Phulwa. Inside the courtroom, the solitary clerk sitting with a female steno is in panic and trying to contact the police.)

First Hetero : Repeal Section 377!
Second Hetero : Stop discrimination against heterosexuals!
Third Hetero : Police Commissioner!
Chorus : *Hai Hai!*
Third Hetero : Prime Minister!
Chorus : *Hai Hai!*
Third Hetero : Law Minister!
Chorus : *Hai Hai!*

(Inside the courtroom, the clerk is speaking urgently on the phone.)

Court Clerk : Get me the Police Commissioner's office *(Pause)*... Yes, is this the Police Commissioner?... Sir, there is a big demonstration taking place just outside the court premises.
Second Hetero : *Jo hum se takrayega...*
Chorus : *Chur Chur ho jayega!*

Enter Vivek, Virender *and two other lathi-wielding constables.*

Vivek : Ho, what goes on over here?

Third Hetero	: (Shouts) High Court!
Chorus	: Hai hai!
Viren	: Look here, you better stop all this shouting or else...
Third Hetero	: Police Commissioner
Chorus	: Hai hai!

(Constables start swinging their lathis about and chase the demonstrators out of the building.)

(Enter Mela Malani *with her munshi and typist,* Kala *and* Swasthi *in the courtroom. They take up their seats on the first row. There is a huge wall clock hanging inside the courtroom on one of the walls, ticking away.)*

Swasthi	: I wonder which judge will come today to hear our case. Justice Bhagwanti or Justice Jack.
Kala	: I'm sure it will be Justice Bhagwanti. That woman is always lucky.
Swasthi	: Who? Lekha?
Kala	: No, silly. Obviously I mean her.

(A gong sounds. Enter Justice Jack *from the rear side of the courtroom. He takes his seat.)*

Justice Jack	: *(Addressing the court clerk)* Get me some coffee. I will hear the cases which were to come up in the morning as well as those in the afternoon session. Justice Bhagwanti is unwell and laid up in bed with a fever and won't be coming for a few days. Court clerk, you may take out the file of the first case listed for the day and give it to me so that I can glance through it before the counsel address their arguments.

(Court clerk hands the files to the judge and sends the steno for some coffee for the judge.)

Swasthi	: Oh my God! It's Justice Jack.
Kala	: Now all our preparations are going to go waste.

Swasthi : Yes. He is not going to listen to a constitutional challenge to Section 377. What will she do now?

(Outside the courtroom Vivek *and* Virender *have returned with two prisoners on whose shirts are written 'Alif Bachpan' and 'Lekha'. The prisoners are both unisexually attired in prison dress. Srinivas, the photojournalist is busy taking photographs of the couple from different, crazy angles. There is* Yani, *a woman journalist from the respected television channel Vista News with a technician who has put a mike in front of* Alif *and is firing questions at him.)*

Yani : Mr. Bachpan, do you have anything to say in your defence?

Alif : All I can say is that I am not guilty.

Yani : And Ms. Lekha? What do you have to say?

Lekha : Exactly what my colleague, Mr. Bachpan has already said. Neither of us is guilty of having committed a crime.

Yani : How can that be, Mr. Bachpan, Sir? There are photographs.

Alif : I'm telling you, Madam, this is a bloody frame-up.

Yani : Why should anyone be interested in framing either of you on such a serious criminal charge?

Lekha : Jealousy. What else?

Alif : Also don't forget that because of this case, my fan following has dropped and I'm no longer the number one star in the film industry and neither is Lekha.

Lekha : Yes. Our market prices have plummeted too.

Yani : But Mr. Bachpan, Madam Lekha, when you say that this whole case is a frame-up, are you saying that the photographs have been doctored?

Alif : *(Cautiously)* Look Yani, with due respect to the members of your tribe, these days journalists write just about anything. They print ten thousand word interviews with stars without ever having met them.

Lekha : And please don't say this doesn't happen, Yani. In this last month I've read two 'exclusive' interviews of myself in two, separate magazines, in which I haven't said one word that was printed. Do you understand, Yani? Not one word. I haven't even met the gentlemen who claim to have interviewed me.

Alif : Look Yani, you are one of the senior journalists associated with one of the more respected and impartial news channels, that is why we are talking to you.

Lekha : Have you seen what some of the gutter press has been writing about us now, at the instance of our rivals? This is becoming a trial by media. I'm not going to leave these people once this is over.

Alif : Yani, you know that millions of purees are involved in various film projects because of this damned case. And yet, the press is just trying to sensationalize the whole thing further.

Yani : Mr. Bachpan, I can promise you that our channel will not do any of this. I accept that you are saying that some of the kids who are in journalism these days tend to let their imagination run wild, and they even fabricate things, but...

Lekha : What do you mean by 'but' Yani? Tell me something, these last three months, before we got embroiled in this case, haven't all the film magazines and gossip channels gone crazy reporting this torrid love affair I'm supposed to be having with Tridevi?

Alif : And likewise, haven't they been linking me up with Binod? In Lekha's case they even wrote that a secret wedding had been planned.

Yani : *(Pacifyingly)* What you are saying is quite true, Sir. And I also appreciate the point which you are making, Madam Lekha.

Lekha : *(Furious)* Tell me how can you reconcile the two stories? My supposed affair with Tridevi with these latest allegations involving me and Alif? And both the stories have been published by the same magazine.

Alif : It's perfectly obvious that at least one of the stories is false, because they both contradict each other, do they not? As a matter of fact both of them are false, completely false.

Lekha : I mean, with a magazine like that what else can you expect? Certainly, nothing even remotely resembling the truth.

Yani : Madam, Sir, I accept all that you have been saying... but in that case, are the photographs fake? Is this a case of trick photography? The police surely wouldn't have progressed in this case without having done forensic tests to make sure the photographs were genuine.

Lekha : No comment.

Yani : *(Persisting)* If the photos are false and the police have made a false case out of them, then you could sue the Government and the magazine for a million purees.

Alif : *(Grimly)* We may yet do that.

Yani : So, is that going to be your line of defence? That the photos are fake?

Alif : No comment.

Lekha : Our lawyer has advised us to say nothing on the subject.

Yani : Is it true that the famous criminal lawyer Mela Malani will be defending both of you in this case?

Alif : That is correct.

(Inside the courtroom, Ms. Mela Malani *has finished studying the book.)*

Mela : Mr. Swasthi.

Swasthi : *(Looks around dazed)* Did someone call out my name?

Mela : *(Louder)* Mr. Swasthi!

Swasthi : Yes, Ma'am.

Mela : Will you please come here?

(He goes to her.)

Swasthi : What are we going to do now, Ma'am?

Mela : We will do something. They don't call me Mela Malani the great criminal lawyer for nothing. Listen to me carefully. There is only one way now. The constitutional challenge arguments are out. We have got to plead guilty and say that the crime was committed during a momentary fit of insanity. Understand. Go outside and explain this to Alif and Lekha.

(Swasthi *goes outside and explains things to* Alif *and* Lekha *after taking them aside.)*

Swasthi : Mr. Bachpan, can I have a word with you? There is a message for you and Madam Lekha from Ms. Malani.

Alif : Yes, what is it?

Swasthi : Only for your ears, sir, and Madam's.

Alif : *(To Yani)* Please excuse me for a minute.

Virender : *(Standing quietly next to* Alif *and* Lekha *suddenly comes to life)* Hey, Mr. Bachpan, you can't go away now.

Swasthi : *(Recognizing Virender)* You again! Are you making trouble again?

Virender : Oh, Mr. Lawyer. *(Thinks)* All right, you may confer but please do it fast.

(Swasthi *takes* Alif Bachpan *aside and whispers in his ear. All the while* Virender, Lekha *and* Yani's *eyes are trained on them.* Yani *is straining desperately to hear a word of what is being said.)*

Alif : Yes, yes I understand perfectly. Let's tell Lekha also, shall we? *(Shouts)* Lekha!

(Lekha *goes and joins them briefly.* Alif *whispers something into her ear.)*

Swasthi : All right then. I'm going back to the court.

(Alif *and* Lekha *take up their former positions, outside the Courtroom, next to* Virender *and* Yani. *Meanwhile, inside the Courtroom, the judge has finished his reading of the case.)*

Justice Jack : Court clerk. Call out the first case now.
Court Clerk : *(Loudly)* State versus Alif Bachpan and Lekha.

(Outside the Courtroom.)

Virender : Please Sir, please Madam, we have to go in now.
Yani : One last question, Mr. Bachpan. Is it true that Ms. Mela Malani is charging you one crore purees for this case?
Alif : No comment.
Lekha : You know very well that good lawyers don't come cheap.
Court Clerk : *(Shouts again)* State versus Alif and Lekha. *Hazir ho*!
Virender : No more questions. We have to go in now. *(To* Yani*)* Sorry Madam, you are not allowed in with your camera.

(The prisoners are brought in by Virender *and* Vivek *and made to stand in the dock.* Ms. Malani *stands up and moves closer to the dias.)*

Justice Jack : Yes, counsel. What do you have to say? This appears to be really an open and shut case.
Prosecutor : Your Lordship is very right. There is absolutely no merit in this appeal.
Mela : *(Angrily)* Of course, merit is there. *(Addressing the Judge)* Your Honour, you will kindly excuse me, but there are several points worth examining in this matter.
Justice Jack : *(Impatiently)* What is there to examine? Let me make it very clear that I'm not interested in any high falutin medical studies or pronouncements on the subject of heterosexuality being normal, so we can leave those aside.
Mela : Please, Your Lordship.
Justice Jack : And don't show me any of the case or law from that sister planet, Uroland. I personally believe our culture is quite different from theirs and in many ways, vastly superior too. What holds true for them

may not necessarily hold true for us. I grant you that we can learn from them in many respects, maybe concerning cyber law or space law, but no, not with respect to laws, concerning the settled, stable society we have in Gayland. Do I make myself clear?

Mela : Please, Your Lordship.

Justice Jack : Ms. Malani, this is an open and shut case. Are you planning to challenge the constitutional validity of Section 377, GPC? Let me inform you that I have heard all those equality arguments before. Frankly, they don't hold any water.

Mela : No, Your Honour. It is not my intention to challenge the constitutional validity of the provision.

Justice Jack : *(Surprised)* Isn't it?

Prosecutor : *(Shocked)* it isn't!

Justice Jack : What other line of argument can possibly be taken in this case, Counsel? Criminal prosecutions under Section 377 generally fail for want of evidence, because the crime is generally committed in collusion, secrecy and darkness and moreover there is no complainant or victim of the crime as the term is commonly understood. However in this case there is clear photographic evidence of the crime having been committed. Surely you don't mean to suggest that the photographs which have been filed are false?

Prosecution : Please, Your Lordship. It is impossible that the photographs could be false. Mr. Srinivas is a very senior and respected journalist. He has stated before the trial court and it has stood the test of strenuous cross examination. Moreover, the expert from the Government laboratory has appeared as a witness and testified that he has carefully examined the negatives of the photographs which were filed in court by the police. He has confirmed that these photographs are as per the negatives and have not been tampered with at all.

Justice Jack : *(Interrupting)* Yes, yes Mr. Prosecutor. We know all that already from the record. Let us hear what Ms. Malani has to say.

Mela : I do not dispute the constitutional validity of Section 377. Neither do I dispute the occurrence of the crime.

Justice Jack : I fail to understand you, Ms. Malani. What else is needed? They have to be punished if they have committed the crime. Whether it took place by consent or not is immaterial for the purposes of this section. Punishment has to follow.

Mela : No, Your Honour. I submit that the act was committed by Mr. Bachpan and Ms. Lekha under a temporary fit of insanity.

Justice Jack : A fit of insanity! Kindly explain yourself more clearly, Ms. Malani. The two prisoners standing here in front of me appear to be perfectly sane.

Mela : Yes, Milord. They are sane. That is why I used the expression 'temporary fit of insanity'. However the background to the crime needs to be appreciated. A few weeks prior to the alleged incident, Mr. Bachpan had been approached by one Mr. Rajesh Bhatt, a well known film maker and director of off beat movies to play the role of a heterosexual in one of his films. Mr. Bachpan was simply rehearsing this role and Ms. Lekha was giving him her cooperation by similarily pretending to have heterosexual tendencies. Now during the rehearsal they became so involved in the characters they were imagining themselves to be that in a momentary fit of insanity they imagined that they were the characters themselves and they committed the sordid act!

Justice Jack : Good God! Is that how it happened?

Prosecutor : I object, Your Honour. This is simply a cooked up story.

Mela : Your Honour may turn to page 86 of the paper book and see the photocopy of the agreement between Alif and Mr. Bhatt in respect of this off beat movie. I have also filed Mr. Bhatt's affidavit in page 92.

Justice Jack : *(Flipping through the pages of the court file)* ... Yes ... They seem to be there.

Prosecutor : Your Lordship, Ms. Malani is being very clever. All this is simply a tissue of lies.

Justice Jack : Mr. Prosecutor, please control yourself. Ms. Malani is a Senior Counsel and an officer of this Court. I have gone through the annexures and the story seems plausible. Is this what really happened Ms. Malani?

Mela : Your Lordship, this is exactly what happened. Everybody knows how creative artistes get carried away by their imagination. I beg leave to quote from one of our classics. *(Quotes)* 'Lovers and mad men have such seething brains/Such shaping fantasies, that apprehend/More than cool reason ever comprehends/The Lunatic, the lover and the poet,/Are of imagination all compact.'[46]

It is clear as daylight Your Honour that both Mr. Bachpan and Lekha were so involved in the character of the persons they were playing that they forgot themselves momentarily.

Justice Jack : *(In a natural voice)* Well, this explains it. Let me tell you Ms. Malani that I am quite frankly an admirer of Mr. Bachpan and have really enjoyed watching some of his movies. I am extremely unhappy to see him like a prisoner. I was shocked when I heard of this incident. This explains it. *(Addressing Alif)* Is this what happened, Mr. Bachpan?

Alif : *(Sheepishly)* Yes, Your Honour.

Justice Jack : *(Addressing Lekha)* Is this what really happened, Ms. Lekha?

Lekha : *(Meekly)* Yes, Your Honour.

Justice Jack : Very well. Is there anything you wish to add, Ms. Malani?

Mela : No, Your Honour. The defence rests its case.

Prosecutor : Your Honour, I object ...

Justice Jack : I have heard your objections, Mr. Prosecutor. Be sure that I will consider them when I am passing judgement on this matter. Court Steno, kindly take down the order.

Steno : *(Picking up a pen and pad)* Yes, Milord.

Justice Jack : *(Dictating)* Present, Public Prosecutor for the State, Ms. Mela Malani, Senior Advocate for the accused persons. I have heard carefully the arguments addressed by counsels for both the parties. Case to come up for passing of judgement after three weeks. In the meantime, the prisoners Mr. Bachpan and Lekha are released on bail subject to their furnishing personal bonds in the appropriate amount before the concerned Magistrate.

Mela : *(With a triumphant expression)* Thank You, Milord.

Justice Jack : The Court shall now adjourn for ten minutes.

(Exit Ms. Malani, Alif, Lekha, the Public Prosecutor, Swasthi, Kala, munshi, clerks *and* Justice Jack *(who goes out through a rear exit.) Outside the courtroom press photographers are clicking away. The Alif Fan Club and Lekha Fan Club are distributing sweets. The general atmosphere is one of celebration and victory.)*

ACT THREE

Scene V

Kala's apartment

(Swasthi *is packing.)*

Swasthi : Whatever you say, Ms. Malani has brains. Yesterday when Justice Jack appeared in Court instead of Justice Bhagwanti, for a minute, I thought everything was lost.

Kala : Yes, Bhagwanti is a real dear. Very indulgent and liberal. She would have listened very patiently to all the arguments we had spent so many hours preparing challenging the constitutional validity of Section 377.

Swasthi : Justice Jack appeared to be rather conservative.

Kala : Yes, he is a bit of a stiff character, isn't he?

Swasthi : That idea about temporary insanity was a stroke of genius. I think we are going to get a favourable verdict.

Kala : *(Visibly annoyed at the praise)* Yes, I suppose she is not so stupid all the time. Do you know what a mean woman she is? She has charged Alif and Lekha one lakh purees each for conducting the case. Yesterday in the evening after arguments in Court they presented her with a gold necklace. If the day after tomorrow they get an acquittal or remission of sentence they will probably give her a suitcase full of gold. Yet what has she given us for all the hard work and preparation for the case? Nothing. Not even a word of thanks!

Swasthi : *(Closing his suitcase)* All these seniors are the same. Even my senior on my planet is like that. Before leaving he told me that he will be deducting wages for the time I have been away from the planet. It's like being a daily wage earner.

Kala : Worse. It's like bonded labour.

Swasthi : I'm going to miss you.

Kala : So am I. Give me a hug.

(He gives her a hug.)

Kala : Tell me, after how many days will you reach your planet?

Swasthi : *(Looks at his watch)* I think this flight takes three days to reach.

Kala : I tell you what I'll do. The judgement in the Alif case is expected the day after tomorrow. As soon as it is out, I will e-mail a copy to you. Okay?

Swasthi : That will be great! *(Regretfully)* I'm so sorry to leave, but I suppose I have to.

Kala : Yes, your Spouse will be missing you. He will be happy to see all the presents you have brought for him.

Swasthi : *(In a sad voice)* Yes, I suppose so.

Kala : I see you've spent a lot on perfumes and colognes. I wonder why you haven't bought a single suit length for your partner. I thought you said he is very keen on dressing well.

Swasthi : *(Thinking quickly)* Actually I wasn't too sure of his preferences. Rather than buy something he doesn't like, I thought it would be better to keep the money unspent and let him buy what he likes on Earth.

Kala : Oh, I see. So that's the explanation. I was wondering about it, especially since you have picked up quite a few dresses for women.

Swasthi : Those are for my ... my niece.

Kala : Your niece? But the dresses are for a woman. Don't tell me you have such a grown-up niece.

Swasthi : Oh, she is very well-built for her age.

Kala : Well, I guess you must be really fond of her, because I noticed that you have bought her at least two dresses which are rather on the expensive side.

Swasthi : Which one did you like more the blue-sequinned dress or the pink pinafore?

Kala : The blue one I think. I'm quite tired of pink, it's become too common.

Swasthi : I'm so glad you liked the blue one because that's for you, not my niece.

Kala : Oh, Swasthi, you shouldn't have! It's too expensive.

Swasthi : Kala, please don't forget that the only reason I have been able to buy these dresses is because you so very generously offered to let me stay with you. Had I stayed on at the Gaylord Hotel, the room rates are so high, I would have been flat broke by now. But it is not for this reason that I bought that dress for you. Nothing can be sufficient tribute to your various kindnesses. This dress here (he takes it out of a packet) is only a very small token of the genuine affection and love which I have developed for you during the course of these past few weeks.

Kala : *(Examining the dress)* Oh, Swasthi, it's beautiful! I loved the dress the moment I set my eyes on it, and to think that you had kept it for me only.

Swasthi : Kala, will you do me a favour?

Kala : Yes, Swasthi.

Swasthi : Could you gift me your pink blouse? The one you wore the day we went to the public park.

Kala : Yes, of course, but what will you do with it? Let me guess. You want to give it to that favourite niece of yours?

Swasthi : That's right. I want to take it as a remembrance. Everytime I see her wearing it, I shall be reminded of you.

Kala : Oh, Swasthi, how sentimental you are! But I'm still worried about your spouse. From what you've told me about him, I think he might be upset that you haven't even picked up a few shirts for him. What's his size, by the way?

Swasthi : About the same as mine.

Kala : Oh, then you can wear each other's clothes once in a while at least. That's a saving.

Swasthi : That's true.

Kala : This throws a different light on his obsession with clothes. Maybe it's because he wants you to look smart as well.

Swasthi : *(Scratching his head)* I suppose that might be the case.

Kala : *(Laughs)* There's a big advantage of marrying a spouse who is the same size as you are. But if you are of the same size I don't see why you should be worried that he may not like that you've bought for him. If he doesn't like the clothes you've bought him, you just keep them for your own use!

Swasthi : *(Hastily)* Oh, I already have enough clothes!

Kala : I don't think that's true. In any case I've bought five shirts for you.

Swasthi : *(Embarrassed)* Oh, Kala, you should not have bothered!

Kala : But I like you Swasthi, and I too would like to give you something. Here, these are for you. *(Takes out a few shirts out of packets and tosses them at Swasthi)* I hope you like them.

Swasthi : *(Fervently)* Oh, I do! I do!

Kala : Mind it you don't give all of them to your spouse. After all you're the guy who's going to work everyday, while he just sits at home. You must keep at least three of these shirts for your own use. Will you promise to do that?

Swasthi : *(Laughs)* I'll probably keep all the shirts for myself.

Kala : Now you're joking. In these few days that we have lived together, I have begun to feel as if I have known you all my life. You're far too considerate of the other person's needs to do anything like that, Swasthi dear. I know you only too well now.

Swasthi : And I feel that I have never before in my life met someone as wonderful and beautiful as you are.

Kala : You say these things with such sincere expressions on your face that I almost think that you actually believe the things you say.

Swasthi : *(Looking hurt)* I do believe them, Kala. I do.

Kala : Shall I tell you something? Before I met you apart from the fact that I had never met Miss Right, I believe I was too individualistic. Somewhere at the back of my mind was also this thought that I don't need a spouse. Let me just concentrate on my career. Now, after having lived with you, I've begun to realize the importance of companionship, of someone to share your sorrows and happiness. I'm going to try and settle down with a nice girl. Of course it'll be difficult to find a girl who is as nice as you are. See, I'm sounding sincere as well, because I mean what I'm saying ... Oh, Swasthi! how I wish sometimes that ... *(changes the topic)* your spouse Swasthi, he must be loving you a lot.

Swasthi : *(Mournfully)* Yes, I suppose so.

Kala : If only I could find a woman like you, I would have married her.

Swasthi : *(To the audience)* If only I were a woman.
Kala : I'm going to miss you.
Swasthi : So am I. Give me a hug.

(She hugs him.)

Swasthi : If you were a man, I would have divorced my spouse and married you.
Kala : Don't say that! Anyway, that's impossible, is it? Have a good trip, and give my love to your spouse.
Swasthi : I'll do that. Bye.
Kala : Bye.

(They hug once again. Exit Swasthi.*)*

ACT FOUR
Scene I
House of Swasthi

Sangeeta : *(Talking to herself)* He had said that he would be returning today from that planet with the strange name. I have actually been missing him. Without him, there is nobody to shout at, nobody to bully. Life seems meaningless. I don't even have any religious books to read these days. Wait, there is someone knocking at the door. Perhaps it is him.

(She opens the door to reveal Swasthi *carrying a suitcase in one hand and packages in the other arm.)*

Swasthi : Hello, my dear!
Sangeeta : *(In a welcoming tone)* Come in. Come in. Are all those packages full of presents for me, my darling?
Swasthi : Yes, yes, I'm feeling so tired.

(He comes inside and slumps down on a sofa.)

Sangeeta : Oh, you poor darling! It must have been a very long and tiring journey, but you're looking quite well, you know.

Swasthi : *(Wearily)* Am I?

Sangeeta : Yes, you are. Your skin is simply glowing. *(Goes close to him and touches his face)* Yes, you re not looking so sickly any more. Looks like they took good care of you on this planet.

Swasthi : Yes, Ms. Malani's junior really took good care of me.

Sangeeta : Who?

Swasthi : My senior's junior.

Sangeeta : Oh, you stayed with him, did you?

Swasthi : *(Hesitates)* Yes.

Sangeeta : *(Examining him closely)* It would not be wrong to say that you are in the pink of health. This is much better than going to any of those health and fitness clubs which have sprung up all over the city. Next time you must take me along as well. Will you promise to do that, my darling?

Swasthi : I promise, I promise. *(Suddenly alert)* No, no, it's quite impossible. We'll be arrested.

Sangeeta : *(Indignant)* You will be arrested for taking me with you?

Swasthi : Yes, yes, your spouse has to be a man.

Sangeeta : *(Laughs shrilly)* A man? Oh, my poor husband, what has happened to you Are you in your senses? Have you been working too hard? *(Suddenly suspicious)* Or have you perhaps drunk too many free cocktails on your flight back home? *(Concerned again)* Now just relax, my dear. I'll go and make you a hot cup of tea right now.

Swasthi : Thank you.

Sangeeta : *(Cannot however resist opening the packets)* But first let me quickly see what is there in these packets. *(Takes out a blouse from the first packet)* Oh, what a wonderfully embroidered blouse! And it's in shocking pink, the colour I wanted. *(Turns sentimental)* You remembered! Now what is there in this packet. *(Opens the second packet)* A pink dress as well! Looks wonderfully expensive too! The colony women are going to die of jealousy.

Swasthi : There are three more packets inside the holdall.

Sangeeta : *(Takes out some lingerie from a third packet)* Oh, how lovely! Such pretty colour too! Now, what's inside this fourth packet? Perfumes! So many bottles! Oh, how nice!

Swasthi : Tell me, my dear. Is there any e-mail for me from that planet.

Sangeeta : No, darling. Nothing at all.

Swasthi : *(To himself)* Strange! She had said she would send me an e-mail with regard to the decision in the case of Alif Bachpan and Lekha.

Sangeeta : Now let me see what is there in this fifth packet. *(Opens it)* Sandals... and gold bangles too. Wonderful! Thank you, my darling. Now I'll go and make a hot cup of tea for you.

(She goes out, humming a tune merrily.)

Swasthi : *(To himself)* What's come over her? I cannot believe that this is my spouse who is calling me darling and making a cup of hot tea for me. *(To the audience)* Do you think her brains have perhaps got scrambled?

(There is a sound of someone knocking on the door. Swasthi *goes and opens it. It's the postman.)*

Postman : There is an e-mail for you, Sir.

Swasthi : I have been expecting an e-mail. Does it say from where?

Postman : Let me see, Sir... It's from some planet called Gayland, Here.

Swasthi : *(Takes the e-mail from him)* Thank you very much.

Postman : Not at all, Sir. Please sign here.

(Swasthi *makes his signature on a register and closes the door.)*

(Exit Postman.)

Swasthi : *(To himself)* This must be the Court order Kala had promised to send. Oh, there is a letter from her as well. *(Reads aloud)*

'Dear Swasthi,
I hope you had a safe and comfortable journey. I am sending you a copy of the court order received just now in the case under Section 377, GPC as promised.
I'm missing you already, more than I can tell. See if you can make a trip again sometime. Give my love to your spouse.
Lots of love,
Kala.'

(Kala's *voice comes over while the letter is being read.)*

Swasthi : Oh, Kala. How I miss you too! Now let me read what the judgement says *(reads the order. Justice Jack's voice comes on).*
'In view of the material which has been placed before us indicating that the accused persons, two highly educated and cultured individuals were suffering from mental aberration when they committed the offence and that as a result of this conviction they will suffer serious consequences to their career, we reduce the sentence to the period already undergone.[47] Justice Jack'.

(Sangeeta *comes in carrying a tray with a plate full of biscuits and a cup of tea.* Swasthi *immediately hides the o-mail in his trouser pocket.)*

Sangeeta : Here, my darling. This tea will do you some good. Tell me something, my dear, what religion do they practice on this planet?

Swasthi : Why do you assume that they have a religion? All planets don't need to have one.

Sangeeta : Yes, they do, Lawyer *sahib*. It's a basic human impulse.

Swasthi : Let me try and remember. *(Thinks)* No, I'm perfectly sure that they don't have any religion.

Sangeeta : Still there must be someone they follow or believe in.

Swasthi : Yes, they do. Someone called King Sol. He was a great revolutionary leader who saved the planet from destruction. I believe that he said and wrote many things. Compilations of his thoughts are available in most bookstores.

Sangeeta : And you of course never bothered to read them? But tell me, do they believe in and follow whatever this King Sol of theirs has said.

Swasthi : Yes, of course.

Sangeeta : Then, he is their religious leader. I told you they must be having a religion. It's very simple. Religion is a matter of faith, not of reason. If they follow him with blind faith, then it is religion; otherwise not. Oh, I wish you had brought something of his for me to read.

Swasthi : Hadn't you started some new religious text when I left?

Sangeeta : Yes, I was reading a religious scripture, but now I've finished it, and I need something else. One of those compilations of King Sol's thoughts would have been lovely.

Swasthi : I'm not so sure that you would have liked it, you know.

Sangeeta : What do you know? Have you read a religious book in your life? Anyhow, it doesn't really matter that you forgot. The main thing is that you're back safe and sound. I've been missing you very much, did you know that?

Swasthi : Yes, yes.

Sangeeta : *(Coyly)* Did you miss me?

Swasthi : *(Starts guiltily)* Yes, of course.

Sangeeta : Did you think of me often?

Swasthi : Of course, my dear.

Sangeeta : *(Satisfied)* You haven't changed at all. Thank God you haven't picked up one of those foreign accents. And me, do you see any change in me?

Swasthi : *(Looks her up and down)* No, I don't think so. Why?

Sangeeta : *(A little upset)* Oh, you haven't noticed! I have a completely different hairstyle now. The hair dresser charged three hundred rupees, and I did this only for you!

Swasthi : For me? But why?

Sangeeta : Silly boy. Can't you understand anything? Tomorrow is my birthday, you remember that, don't you?

Swasthi : *(Hastily)* Yes, yes.

Sangeeta : *(Smiling)* So we'll lie in bed all day long.

Swasthi : *(In a tone of panic)* No, we can't do that!

Sangeeta : *(Pouting)* Why, do you have to got to your silly courts tomorrow as well? And to think that you've returned only today.

Swasthi : *(Staring into space like a madman)* It's not allowed! It's against the law!

Sangeeta : *(Disconcerted)* Against the law? To stay at home after such a long journey. What's happening to you, my dear? *(Snaps her fingers)* Oh, I know what! You're experiencing a reverse culture shock. That's why you're making all these funny remarks, which I don't understand. You must relax at home tomorrow, my dear. You need at least two, three days to adjust to the old ways of our planet. Here, why don't you have these nice chocolate biscuits with your tea? I brought some especially for you. And do you want something else as well?

Swasthi : *(Sipping the tea)* Something else? What else could I want?

Sangeeta : *(To the audience)* After one month of being away from me, he asks, 'What else could I want?'

*(*Sangeeta *comes close and kisses him.)*

Swasthi : Don't do that. Someone may be watching.

Sangeeta : So what?

Swasthi : You don't understand. It's a crime. We may get arrested and have to go to jail.

Sangeeta : Oh, my poor darling! You have been working so hard. Do you want me to press your head?

Swasthi : No, no.

Sangeeta : *(To the audience)* Do you think his brain has perhaps got scrambled? If I kiss him will we get arrested and go to jail?

Swasthi : *(Yawns)* Now I am feeling sleepy.

Sangeeta : I have kept a freshly-ironed kurta pyjama set in the bathroom for you, my dear. Go and change. I'm also going to bed.

(Sangeeta *climbs into bed.* Swasthi *goes to change. After a while he comes out of the bathroom and goes and lies down on the carpet.)*

Sangeeta : What are you doing there?

Swasthi : I am going to sleep.

Sangeeta : Sleep! On the carpet. Are you all right?

Swasthi : *(Stubbornly)* I always sleep on the carpet.

Sangeeta : *(Peremptorily)* Come on up!

Swasthi : No.

Sangeeta : Why ever not?

Swasthi : It's a crime.

Sangeeta : No, it's not.

Swasthi : Yes, it is.

(After a few minutes Sangeeta *comes down from the bed and lies down on the carpet next to* Swasthi.*)*

Swasthi : Why have you come here?

Sangeeta : I have been reading in the same scripture that if the mountain cannot go to a person then he or she must go to the mountain.

NOTES

1. Following publicity given to the *Brown* case, the Law Commission in the UK was asked to carry out an extensive enquiry into the issue of consent in criminal law with special reference to sado-masochistic conduct. (Law Commission Consultation Paper No.

139, Consent in the Criminal Law, *HMSO, 1995, Appendix C.*) Mr. Paul Roberts, advising the Law Commission on the philosophical foundations of consent and the criminal law concluded that 'there is no intelligible answer to the question (or riddle) : to what level of injury should consent be effective in protecting the injured from criminal liability.' In a recent decision, the European Court of Human Rights has upheld the verdict in *Brown* of an English Court that irrespective of consent, sado-masochistic conduct would go against the criminal law of the land.

2. Report titled 'Gay Fathers Make Better Dads', published in *The Times Higher Education Supplement*, Dec 31, 1999.
3. From the world classic, *Gitagovinda of Jayadeva : Love Song of the Dark Lord.* Translated from the original Sanskrit by Barbara Stoler Miller, Columbia University Press, 1977.
4. *Ibid.*
5. *Ibid.*
6. *Ibid.*
7. Reference is to the XYZ case decided by the European Court of Human Rights.
8. This is a direct quote from paras 12 and 13 of the aforesaid judgement, apart from a few words necessary to invert the facts.
9. Again a direct quote from para 32 of the aforesaid judgement.
10. The cities named in *The Books of Genesis* are Sodom and Gomorrah. The angels are male in the original text, and the virtuous resident whose life is sought to be spared is named Lot. Also in the original text, it is Abraham and not King Sol.
11. Extracted with minor alterations from *The Book of Genesis.*
12. *Ibid.* The newly inserted words are given in brackets.
13. *Ibid.* the capital letters are mine, used for emphasis, and are not there in the original text.
14. *Ibid.*
15. Section 377 of the Gayland Penal Code reproduced here is in fact identical to Section 377 of the Indian Penal Code.
16. The Explanation to Section 377 of the Gayland Penal Code here is in fact identical to that of the Explanation to Section 377 of the Indian Penal Code.
17. Article 14 of the Constitution of Gayland as produced is in fact identical to Article 14 of the Constitution of India, except for the single word in brackets.
18. In fact in this case the Supreme Court of India has held that the right to privacy is part and parcel of the right to life and liberty enshrined in Article 21 of the Constitution of India.

19. This is an extract from the petition filed by the Aids Bhedbhav Virodhi Andolan in the Delhi High Court titled *ABVA versus Union of India and others*. For the purpose of this play, certain words have been replaced with their antonyms and very few other new words introduced/replaced, otherwise the text remains unchanged.
20. *Ibid.*
21. The organisation being referred to is actually Amnesty International. This modified extract is also taken from the ABVA petition.
22. This extract, modified somewhat is also taken from the ABVA petition.
23. *Ibid.*
24. *Ibid.*
25. As a matter of fact the Kinsey Report gives exactly the reverse figures. According to this report two per cent of women are exclusively lesbian and six per cent of men were homosexual for a substantial part of their lives.
26. The reference here is not to *Boris* but *Norris*. The judgement referred to is the decision of the European Court of Human Rights in the case of *Norris versus Ireland*, decided in 1989. (Ser. A, No.142, 13 EHRR 186).
27. The reference here is not to *Dungeon* but *Dudgeon*. The judgement in the *Dudgeon Case* was delivered by the European Court of Human Rights in 1981. (Ser.A, No. 45, 4 EHRR 149).
28. The facts in *Boris* after being suitably inverted are more or less identical with those in *Norris*. Interested readers can read the actual decision in *Norris*. It is now also available on the Internet.
29. Unaltered extract from *Norris*.
30. Unaltered extract taken from para 30 of the judgement in *Norris*.
31. Extract taken from para 32 of the judgement in *Norris*, (with very minor alterations).
32. Extract taken from para 38 of the judgement in *Norris*, (with very minor alterations).
33. Extract taken from para 42 of the judgement in *Norris*, (with very minor alterations).
34. Extract taken from para 46 of the judgement in *Norris*, (with very minor alterations).
35. *Ibid.* emphasis is mine.
36. *Ibid.* emphasis is mine.
37. This case has actually reference to the case of *Bowers versus Hardwick*, decided by the Supreme Court of the United States in 1986. (478U.S. 186 106 S.Ct. 2841). The facts are more or less similar to those in the fictional case of *Showers versus Sadsack*.

38. Extracted from the judgement of Justice White in *Bowers versus Hardwick* (with very minor alterations).
39. Extracted from the judgement of Justice White in *Bowers versus Hardwick,* with only the name of the city Georgia deleted and one term 'heterosexual intercourse' (given in brackets) substituted for 'homosexual sodomy'.
40. Extracted, with minor modifications, from Chief Justice Burger's concurring judgement.
41. Extracted, with minor modifications, from the dissenting judgement delivered by Justice Blackmun in *Bowers versus Hardwick.* It may be noted that Justice Blackmun was joined by Justices Brennan, Marshall and Stevens.
42. *Ibid.*
43. *Ibid.*
44. *Ibid.*
45. *Ibid.*
46. A famous quotation from Shakespeare's *A Midsummer Night's Dream.*
47. A practically identical order was passed by Justice M.H. Beg, of the Indian Supreme Court in the case of *Chittranjan Das versus State,* a reported decision on Section 377, Indian Penal Code, 1860. (1974 (4) Supreme Court Cases 454).

IN THE HIGH COURT OF DELHI AT NEW DELHI

Civil Writ Petition No. .... of 1994

AIDS Bhedbhav Virodhi Andolan
(AIDS Anti-Discrimination Movement) .....Petitioner

Versus

Union of India and others .....Respondent

INDEX

Sl. No.	*Particulars*	*Pages*	*Court fee*
1.	Urgent application.	1	2.75
2.	Memo of parties.	2	50.00
2A.	List of dates.	2A - 2B	
3.	Writ Petition.	3-18	
4.	Affidavit in support thereof.	19	
5.	Application for interim directions under section 151 C.P.C.	20-27	
6.	Affidavit in support thereof.	28	
7.	Annexure 'A' 'Less Than Gay', A Citizen's Report published by the petitioner on the status of homosexuality in India, 1991.	29-124	
8.	Annexure 'B1', 'B2' and 'B3'. Newspaper clipping from *The Pioneer* dated 10-2-94, *The Pioneer* dated 21-2-94 and *The Sunday* dated 27th March-2nd April, 1994.	125-128	
9.	Annexure 'C' Extracts from 'National AIDS Programme of the NACO,' 1992. *Source* Trip Report, India Oct - Nov 93.	129-130	
10.	Annexure 'D' Article in 'AIDS Action' International newsletter dated Dec. 1993-Feb.'94.	131-132	

Sl. No.	*Particulars*	*Pages*	*Court fee*
11.	Annexure 'E' Extracts from the report 'Amnesty International and Homosexuality', 1987.	133	
12.	Annexure 'F' Extract from the report of the Indian Law Commission, 1837.	134	
13.	Annexure 'G' Article in the *Statesman* dated 1.3.1994.	135-136	
14.	Annexure 'H' Statement of the American Psychiatric Association, 1973. *Source:* 'Less than Gay' report.	137	
15.	Annexure 'I' Statement of the Indian Medical Association, 1994 appearing in *The Pioneer* 14-2-1994.	138	
16.	Annexure 'J' Statement regarding prevalence of homosexuality amongst animals. *Source:* 'Less than Gay' report.	139	
17.	Annexure 'K' Extract from the Kinsey Report, 1948 and 1953. *Source:* 'Less than Gay' report.	140	
18.	Annexure 'L' Extracts from chapter on homosexuality in Vatsyayana's *Kamasutra*. *Source:* 'Less than Gay' report.	141-143	
19.	Annexure 'M' Newspaper article in *The Indian Express*.	144	
20.	Annexure 'N' Copy of 'London Declaration on AIDS Prevention' 1988.	145-147	
21.	Annexure 'O' Vakalatnama	148	2.75

IN THE HIGH COURT OF DELHI AT NEW DELHI

To
The Deputy Registrar
High Court of Delhi
New Delhi

AIDS Bhedbhav Virodhi Andolan ..... Petitioner

Versus

Union of India and others ..... Respondents

URGENT APPLICATION

Dear Sir,

Will you kindly treat the accompanying application as an urgent one in accordance with the High Court rules.

The ground for urgency is: interim directions are prayed for.

Yours faithfully,
AIDS Bhedbhav Virodhi Andolan,
Through

(RAJESH TALWAR)
Advocate
New Delhi 19-4-94

IN THE HIGH COURT OF DELHI AT NEW DELHI

Civil Writ Petition No. .... of 1994

AIDS Bhedbhav Virodhi Andolan
(AIDS Anti-Discrimination Movement) ..... Petitioner

Versus

Union of India and others ..... Respondents

LIST OF DATES

10th February, 1994	News report in *The Pioneer* where the Respondent No. 4 is reported to have said that distributing condoms will mean the acceptance of a crime.
21st February, 1994	Report in *The Pioneer* where the Respondent No. 4 has stated that she considers homosexual to be abnormal, and will not hesitate to step up surveillance to ensure that inmates do not indulge in homosexual activities.
25th February, 1994	Petition filed by Shri Janak Raj Jai, where he has requested the court to issue directions that condoms ought not to be supplied.
27th March, 1994	Respondent No. 4 in an interview with some members of the Petitioner association refused to keep condoms in Tihar jail dispensary without realizing the gravity of the situation.
27th March, 1994	News item in *Sunday* magazine where Respondent No. 4 stated that there is no compelling reason to supply condoms to the inmates of Tihar jail or carry out an AIDS awareness programme.

(Shobha Aggarwal)
(AIDS Bhedbhav Virodhi Andolan)

Through

RAJESH TALWAR
Advocate

IN THE HIGH COURT OF DELHI AT NEW DELHI

Civil Writ Petition No. .... of 1994

In the matter of :

AIDS Bhedbhav Virodhi Andolan ..... Petitioner

Versus

1. Union of India
   through Secretary
   Ministry of Home Affairs
   North Block, New Delhi - 110001

2. Delhi Administration
   through Chief Secretary
   National Capital Territory
   Old Secretariat, Delhi.

3. The District and Sessions Judge
   Tis Hazari Courts, Delhi.

4. Inspector General of Prisons
   Tihar Jail, Delhi.

5. Superintendent of Jail
   Tihar Jail, Delhi.

IN THE HIGH COURT OF DELHI AT NEW DELHI
Civil Writ Petition No. 1745 of 1994

MEMO OF PARTIES
AIDS Bhedbhav Virodhi Andolan, a voluntary association having its office at N 202, Nand Nagri, Delhi-110093, through its member, Ms. Shobha Aggarwal ......Petitioner

Versus

1. Union of India
   through Secretary
   Ministry of Home Affairs
   North Block, New Delhi - 110001.
2. Delhi Administration
   through Chief Secretary
   National Capital Territory
   Old Secretariat, Delhi.
3. The District and Sessions Judge
   Tis Hazari Courts, Delhi.
4. Inspector General of Prisons
   Tihar Jail, New Delhi.
5. Superintendent of Jail
   Tihar Jail, New Delhi.
6. National AIDS Control Organization (NACO)
   Through Director, Red Cross Road,
   Opp. Parliament House,
   New Delhi - 110001. ...Respondents

(Shobha Aggarwal)
AIDS Bhedbhav
Virodhi Andolan

through

RAJESH TALWAR
(Advocate)

New Delhi, 19.4.94.

A WRIT PETITION UNDER ARTICLES 226 AND 227 OF THE CONSTITUTION OF INDIA CHALLENGING THE CONSTITUTIONAL VALIDITY OF SECTION 377 OF THE INDIAN PENAL CODE 1908 AND FOR THE ISSUANCE OF A WRIT IN THE NATURE OF MANDAMUS, CERTIORARI, PROHIBITION OR ANY WRIT, DIRECTION OR ORDER DIRECTING THE RESPONDENTS TO TAKE APPROPRIATE MEASURES IN ORDER TO PREVENT THE SPREAD OF THE DISEASE KNOWN AS AIDS AND THE TARGETING/SEGREGATION OF CERTAIN GROUPS OR INDIVIDUALS

To,

The Hon'ble Chief Justice of the High Court
of Delhi and his companion Justice of the
High Court of Delhi at New Delhi.

The humble petition of the petitioner above named

Most respectfully showeth:

1. That the AIDS Bhedbhav Virodhi Andolan (AIDS Anti-Discrimination Movement) is an association of social activists, professionals and other like-minded and concerned individuals. Established in 1988, its members include teachers, journalists, counsellers, lawyers, doctors and those working for causes such as sexual minorities, drug users, professional blood donors, environment, gender issues, etc. Two ABVA members along with government staff are involved in the distribution of condoms amongst sex workers at Delhi's red light area at G.B. Road for the last four years. ABVA has been regularly meeting the concerned officials of the Delhi Administration, the Union Health Ministry, National Aids Control Organization (NACO), Medical Council of India (MCI), Indian Council of Medical Research (ICMR), WHO, UNDP, World Bank, UN officials based in Delhi, etc.

   The ABVA has brought out a series of citizens reports highlighting the problems of sexual minorities, status of so called high risk groups, etc. These reports are variously titled as (1) Less than Gay (2) Women and AIDS - Denial and Blame (3) Blood of the Professionals (4) This Sugar is Bitter (5) Hard Times for Positive Travel.

   The report titled 'Less Than Gay' focuses on the situation and status of homosexuals and lesbians in India. A copy of this report has been annexed herewith this petition and is marked as Annexure 'A'.

2. That Ms Shobha Aggarwal is a member of the ABVA and has been duly authorized by the association and is competent to sign and file the present writ petition.
3. That in recent weeks several disturbing reports have appeared in the press viz. in *The Pioneer* dated 10th February, 1994 and 21st February and in *Sunday* magazine dated 27th March and 2nd April, 1994 where the respondent No. 4 has taken a certain attitude without caring to consider the detailed horrific consequences and logical fallout of such an attitude. Mrs Kiran Bedi, Inspector General of Prisons has made statements to the effect that:
   (a) the supply of condoms to the inmates of Tihar Jail would amount to encouraging people to indulge in homosexuality. It would be like legalizing drugs.
   (b) the supply of condoms will be a tacit admission that homosexuality is rampant among the prisoners. Homosexuality is a punishable crime under the Indian Penal Code and therefore distributing condoms will mean the acceptance of a crime. A copy of these newspaper items have been annexed herewith and have been marked as Annexure 'B1', 'B2', and 'B3'.
4. That in the light of the statements made by the Respondent No. 4, the petitioner above named fears that the government owned National AIDS Programme is not going to be implemented, condoms are not going to be supplied to prisoners and moreover prisoners who are suspected of being homosexual may be targeted or segregated by the prison authorities or could even be criminally prosecuted under Section 377, hence this present petition.
5. That the petitioner fears that non-distribution of condoms to prisoners will lead to large-scale spread of HIV infection in India. AIDS has assumed alarming proportions. The AIDS pandemic has engulfed India, which has an estimated one million HIV positive persons. As in Africa, the commonest mode of spread of AIDS in India is through unsafe (unprotected with condoms) sexual activity. The other modes

of spread are through the use of contaminated syringes and needles and of infected blood/blood products. India is thus likely to follow the pattern of Sub-Saharan Africa, one-third of which is on its way to devastation because of AIDS. AIDS is fast emerging as a major public health problem in India. To control and prevent the incidence of AIDS in the country, a five-year project funded by the World Bank, World Health Organisation and the Government of India got off on 21.09.1992. The World Bank has given $84 million, the WHO $1.5 million and the rest by the Government of India. Since there is no cure for the disease, nor any preventive vaccine available, the only route is to observe necessary precautions, viz., supply of safe blood through blood banks, promote use of condoms, and ensure use of disposable syringes and needles. Details of the programme are annexed herewith and marked.as Annexure 'C'.

6. That preventing HIV transmission in prisons not only protects prisoners, but others in the wider community too. Most inmates are in prison for brief periods only, and return to their home communities when they are released. If they are infected they could pass the virus to others through unsafe drug use or unprotected sex.
7. That surveys have shown that sex between prisoners happen, in spite of severe penalties. For example, between 2 to 30 per cent of inmates in prisons in UK, USA, Australia and Brazil reported sex in prisons which often involves unprotected and intercourse for men. In a survey of 5 prisons in Zambia over 12 per cent of male prisoners reported sexual experience — both forced and consensual. (Article in *AIDS Action International newsletter* dated Dec '93 - Feb '94 is attached herewith and marked as Annexure 'D'.
8. That in fact on a plain reading of Section 377 it becomes clear that homosexuality *per se* is not an offence. An act of sodomy (whether heterosexual or homosexual) can however be classified as a crime under Section 377 of the Indian Penal Code. That the petitioner wishes to make it clear that while we are against forced sexual activity, whether homosexual or heterosexual and strongly protest against it, but consensual

adult homosexual acts cannot be clubbed together with forced homosexual acts.

9. That even if it is assumed that the Respondent No. 4 has taken the position that supply of condoms would run counter to Section 377 of the Indian Penal Code, such a position is not maintainable because according to the petitioner Section 377 is now otiose and must be struck down by this Court as being unconstitutional and violative of the fundamental rights guaranteed to every citizen of India for the following amongst other reasons:
   (a) because in Kharak Singh's case decided by the Supreme Court of India it has been held that the right to privacy is part and parcel of the fundamental right to life and liberty guaranteed by Article 21 of the Constitution. Article 21 has also been given a very wide interpretation in the case of *Francis Coralie vs Union of India* (AIR 1981 SC 746) wherein the Court observed though Justice Bhagwati (page 753) that 'we think that the right to life includes the right to live with human dignity and all that goes along with it.... Every act which offends or impairs human dignity would constitute deprivation *pro tanto* of this right to live.'
   (b) because drafted in 1833 the Indian Penal Code is in many respects archaic and absurd. In 1957 the British Committee on homosexual offences and prostitution under the chairmanship of Sir John Wolfendon recommended that adult consensual homosexual acts be decriminalized. Such a change had been recommended more than 50 years before by Havelock Ellis, eminent British sexologist and author of the path breaking studies in the psychology of sex. Since 1958 the Homosexual Law Reforms Society of Great Britain have campaigned for such a step. National debates centered around the question as to whether the State should regulate morality. This long campaign resulted in decriminalization of private adult homosexual consensual acts in England and Wales through the Sexual Offences Act, 1967.

(c) because India is one of the few countries that continues to keep an anachronistic sodomy law in its books. The British passed such laws in all their colonies. In July, 1990 Hong Kong decriminalized adult consensual homosexual acts. India, Pakistan, Malaysia and Singapore are the only Asian colonies that still have sodomy laws.

(d) because the right to privacy has also been recognized by the various international conventions on human rights. Article 12 of the Universal Declaration of Human Rights, states : 'No one shall be subjected to arbitrary interference with his privacy, family, home or correspondence, nor to attacks upon his honour and reputation.'

(e) because after years of lobbying and negotiation by European gay rights organizations, even a respected international organization like Amnesty International has in recent years taken a stand on homosexuality. The main report of its research project 'Amnesty International and Homosexuality' released in April, 1987 summarized Amnesty's exhaustive research into the persecution of gay people all over the world, but concentrates mainly on imprisonment of gay persons. The main conclusions of the report need to be noted and adopted by the Indian government and civil rights organizations. Extracts of the report are annexed herewith and marked as Annexure 'E'.

(f) because the idea that sexual relations must take place only within a prescribed sexual format shows bias, prejudice, ignorance and lack of tolerance.

(g) because Section 377 is violative of Article 14 of the Constitution since it discriminates against persons purely on the basis of their sexual orientation.

(h) because the expression 'carnal intercourse' used in Section 377 is extremely vague and ambiguous, lending itself to diverse interpretations and for this reason also the section ought to be struck down as unconstitutional. It is pertinent to mention here that this particular

Section was introduced in a rushed manner by the Law Commission in 1937, with practically no debate on the issue. The relevant extract from the Law Commission Report in 1937 is annexed herewith and marked as Annexure 'F'. Many criminologists and law enforcement experts have expressed the view that sexual activities between consenting adults in private, will not be subject to criminal law. In homosexuality the role of the criminal law is excessive. Article in *The Statesman* dated 1.3.1994 is annexed herewith and marked as Annexure G'.

(i) because according to established medical opinion such as the American Psychiatric Association, homosexuality is perfectly normal, reflecting simply a different sexual orientation and pattern of loving and cannot be considered as abnormal any more. A statement by the Association to this effect is annexed herewith and marked as Annexure 'H'.

(j) a statement made by the President, Indian Medical Association, concurring with the American Psychiatric Association is annexed herewith and marked as Annexure 'I'.

(k) because it has been established as a result of scientific investigations that homosexual practices are not peculiar to man alone as thought earlier, but homosexuality is prevalent amongst animals as well. Relevant extracts from well established and documented scientific opinion on the subject is annexed herewith and marked as Annexure 'J'.

(l) because the decision of the Court in this case will have an impact not only on the question as to whether condoms should be supplied in Tihar Jail but whether as a matter of policy, they should be supplied in jails all over the country.

(m) because even outside the specific context in which this petition has been filed, it is essential that the Court declare Section 377 as *ultra vires* of the Constitution in order to protect the fundamental and legal rights of sexual minorities and to ensure that even outside prisons, there is no prosecution of sex workers and persons who have a different sexual orientation.

(n) because according to the Kinsey Report on human sexuality published way back in 1948 to 1953, two per cent of women are lesbians and four per cent of men have been homosexuals for a substantial part of their lives. While the percentage may appear to be small, in practice this means that millions of people all over the globe and even in India possess a different sexual orientation and pattern of loving. A copy of the relevant extracts from the Kinsey Report is annexed herewith and marked as Annexure 'K'.

(o) because it is totally erroneous to suppose that homosexuality is essentially a western phenomenon and is being exported to India. In fact, ancient Indian art and sculpture testifies to the prevalence of homosexuality in this country to a greater or lesser extent.

(p) because even in the *Kamasutra*, an authoritative text on sexuality by the sage Vatsyayana, an entire chapter has been devoted to the subject. A true copy of the same (English translation) is annexed herewith and marked as Annexure 'L'.

(q) that according to Article 25 (1), all persons have been guaranteed freedom of conscience, which must be understood to mean the right to have a certain sexual orientation.

10. That even if it is assumed that this Hon'ble Court does not consider Section 377 to be unconstitutional or *ultra vires* of the Constitution of India, it must still order the respondent to supply condoms to the prisoners without segregating, together with other directions for the prevention of AIDS, for the following amongst other reasons:

(a) because if jail inmates are segregated, tortured and criminally prosecuted purely on the basis of their sexual orientation, it will amount to persecution of a sexual minority which is prohibited under the Constitution as violative of the fundamental rights of these persons.

(b) that segregation of HIV positive prisoners will not help because even if a person has tested HIV negative it does not guarantee that a person is virus free. The body can take between six weeks and a year after infection with the virus to produce the antibodies which show in HIV positive tests. Therefore, if no condoms are distributed then the only way to stop spread of AIDS would be solitary confinement for all the prisoners, which would be inhuman, illegal and impractical.

(c) because the importance of taking steps to prevent the spread of the disease known as AIDS must be fully appreciated. According to Dr Michael Merson, Director of WHO's Global Programme on AIDS, currently India has more HIV infections than any other country of the world. According to WHO estimates if transmission of HIV continues at the same pace, by the year 2000, there will be 5 million infected persons in Delhi alone and the number of AIDS cases would exceed one million. It is well known that in parts of Africa, entire communities have been wiped out by AIDS. Half of the people coming into hospitals in northern Thailand have HIV infection. While the epidemic cannot be stopped, it can certainly be slowed down. Money has to be pumped in for promotion of condoms, educating youth and mass information. A newspaper report which refers to all these facts cited above is annexed herewith and marked as Annexure 'M'.

(d) because the most obvious way to deal with the large scale spread of HIV infection in the jails would be to distribute condoms in the jails. The threat from AIDS in a country like India is too serious for the debate to be clouded by outmoded notions of morality. It would be totally in keeping with public interest if condoms are kept in the dispensary within Tihar Jail where inmates could freely and voluntarily have access to the same. In fact, by means of the London Declaration herewith annexed as Annexure 'N' the Union Government has undertaken to supply condoms free in health care facilities.

(e) because there is no reason to suppose that the incidence of homosexuality would rise on account of the supply of condoms in jails. There is absolutely no nexus between the supply of condoms with the extent of sexual activity that takes place.

(f) because according to the National AIDS Programme, the AIDS pandemic has engulfed India, which has an estimated one million HIV positive persons. As in Africa, the commonest mode of spread of AIDS in India is through unsafe (unprotected with condoms) sexual activity. The other modes of spread are through the use of contaminated syringes and needles and of infected blood/blood products. India is thus likely to follow the pattern of sub-Saharan Africa, one-third of which is on the way to devastation because of AIDS. AIDS is fast emerging as a major public health problem in India (Annexure 'C').

(g) because according to the Directive Principles of State Policy enshrined in Part IV of the Constitution of India, specifically Article 47 it is stated:

'The State shall regard the raising of the level of nutrition and the standard of living of its people and the improvement of public health as among its primary duties, and in particular the State shall endeavour to bring about prohibition of the consumption except for medical purposes of intoxicating drinks and of drugs which are injurious to health.'

(h) because even if this Court determines that Section 377 of the Indian Penal Code is constitutionally valid, even then under the provisions of the Constitution it must direct the Union Government to implement the National AIDS Programme, and direct the respondents to supply condoms to all persons, including prisoners or persons belonging to a sexual minority.

(i) because according to 'AIDS Action' a respected international newsletter on AIDS prevention and control, a recent WHO sponsored report showed that condoms are now available in prisons in over half the countries surveyed, including Brazil, Canada, Costa Rica and many other European countries. A copy of this newsletter is annexed herewith and marked as Annexure 'D'.

(j) because the Union Government has obtained a sum of Rs. 200 crore from the World Bank after signing the London Declaration, which is annexed herewith and marked as Annexure 'N'. According to the agreement, the Union Government is bound to supply condoms to the prisoners failing which the aid granted can be withdrawn forthwith.

(k) because making condoms freely available for the jail inmates is a step in the right direction. This is a scientific method to control the spread of the AIDS epidemic. The provision of disposable syringes should be ensured at the dispensary within the jail premises. Organisations like the National AIDS Control Organization should be consulted in such situations.

(l) because the distribution of condoms amongst prisoners for their protection does not amount to abetment of an offence within the meaning of Section 107 of the Indian Penal Code. The jail authorities would simply be acting in public interest to ensure that a terrible disease does not spread in the prison and outside.

(m) because there should be no further delay in providing condoms at the dispensary in Tihar Jail for inmates in the larger public interest.

(n) because if the position of the Respondent No. 4 is to be accepted, in that case condoms should not be supplied even to sex workers in the red light areas since prostitution is yet to be legalized in the country.

11. That on the basis of certain newspaper clippings one Shri Janak Raj Jai has filed a so-called public interest litigation before this Hon'ble Court registered as Civil Writ No. 1009 of 1994 in which he has taken the line of the Respondent No. 4 to the effect that condoms ought not to be supplied to the inmates of Tihar Jail. Since the subject matter of this petition is in some respects analogous to our case, it is

desirable that this case also be listed and heard before the Division Bench of Justices Saharya and Bhandari who are hearing that case. That petition is due to come up on the 26th of April, 1994.

12. That the petitioner has not filed any other similar petition either before this Hon'ble High Court or before the Supreme Court of India.

PRAYER

In the premises, the petitioner most humbly prays your Lordships to be graciously pleased to issue to the Respondents or each or any of them directions, orders or writs as may be appropriate for enforcing the legal and fundamental rights (conferred by Part III of the Constitution) of the petitioner/jail inmates and for this purpose *inter alia*:

(a) to declare that Section 377 of the Indian Penal Code is unconstitutional and void—

   (1) as being hit by the provisions of Articles 13, 14, 21 and 25 of the Constitution of India.

(b) to direct the implementation of the Government's National AIDS Programme.

(c) to declare that all actions and proceedings purporting to have been done or taken by the respondents and each of them under the said unconstitutional and void law are wholly unauthorized by law, illegal and void and not binding on the jail inmates.

(d) to restrain the respondents from segregating or isolating prisoners with a certain sexual orientation or those suffering from AIDS or from commencing prosecution against those prisoners who are suspected to have participated in consensual anal intercourse.

(e) to direct the respondents to immediately make condoms available at the dispensary within Tihar Jail, where prisoners could freely obtain them without fear that they will be prosecuted on account of their sexual orientation.

(f) to direct that only disposable syringes be used in the dispensary within Tihar Jail.

(g) to direct the jail authorities to regularly consult with the National AIDS Control Organization, namely, the Respondent No. 6.

(h) may pass any other writ, direction or order as this Hon'ble Court deems fit and proper in the circumstances of this case.

Shobha Aggarwal
AIDS Bhedbhav Virodhi Andolan

Through

RAJESH TALWAR
Advocate

New Delhi

EUROPEAN COURT OF HUMAN RIGHTS
CASE OF X, Y AND Z VERSUS THE UNITED KINGDOM
(75/1995/581/667)
JUDGEMENT

STRASBOURG
22 April 1997

The present judgment is subject to editorial revision before its reproduction in final form in the *Reports of Judgments and Decisions* for 1997. These reports are obtainable from the publisher Carl Heymanns Verlag KG Luxembourg Straβe 449, D-50939 Köln), who will also arrange for their distribution in association with the agents for certain countries as listed below.

List of Agents

Belgium: Etablissements Emile Bruylant (rue de la Régence 67, B-1000 Bruxelles)

Luxembourg: Librairie Promoculture (14, rue Duchscher (place de Paris), B. P. 1142, L - 1011 Luxembourg - Gare)

The Netherlands: B. V. Juridische Boekhandel & Antiquariaat A. Jongbloed & Zoon (Noordeinde 39, NL - 2514 GC's - Gravenhage)

SUMMARY

Judgment delivered by a Grand Chamber

(*This summary by the registry does not bind the Court)

United Kingdom— refusal to register post - operative transsexual as father of child born to partner by artificial insemination by donor (Human Fertility and Embryology Act 1990, Children Act 1989)

I. Article 8 of the Convention

A. Existence of 'family life'

Notion of 'family life' not confined solely to families based on marriage — factors such as cohabitation and length of relationship is of relevance.

X lived with Y, to all appearance as her male partner, since 1979 and was associated in treatment leading to artificial insemination by donor ('AID').

Conclusion: **Article 8 applicable (unanimous).**

B. Compliance with Article 8

Wide margin of appreciation since no common European standard with regard to granting of parental rights to transsexuals or manner in which social relationship between child conceived by AID and person performing social role of father should be reflected in law.

Community has interest in maintaining coherent system of family law prioritising best interests of child — unclear whether amendment sought would benefit children conceived by AID or have implications in other areas of family law — in these circumstances State may justifiably be cautious in changing law.

Disadvantages suffered by applicants do not outweigh general interest given facts of case, in particular that X not prevented for acting as Z's father in social sense and could, with Y, apply for joint residence order in respect of her.

Conclusion: **No violation (fourteen votes to six).**

II. Article 14 of the Convention taken together with Article 8

Article 14 complaint tantamount to restatement of Article 8 complaint — no need to re-examine issues.

Conclusion: **Not necessary to consider complaint (seventeen votes to three).**

Court's case-law referred to

13.6.1979, Marckx v. Belgium; 17.10.1986, Rees v. the United Kingdom; 18.12.1986, Johnston and Others v. Ireland; 27.9.1990, Cossey v. the United Kingdom; 25.3.1992, B. v. France; 26.5.1994, Keegan v. Ireland; 27.10.1994, Kroon and Others v. the Netherlands

In the case of X, Y and Z versus the United Kingdom[fn1],

The European Court of Human Rights, sitting in accordance with Rule 51 of Rules of Court A[fn2] as a Grand Chamber composed of the following judges:

Mr R. Ryssdal, President,

Mr R. Bernhardt,

Mr Thór Vilhjálmsson,

Mr F. Matscher,

Mr L.-E. Pettiti,

Mr C. Russo,
Mr A. Spielmann,
Mr J. De Meyer,
Mr N. Valticos,
Mr I. Foighel,
Sir John Freeland,
Mr A. B. Baka,
Mr M. A. Lopes Rocha,
Mr J. Makarczyk,
Mr D. Gotchev,
Mr K. Jungwiert,
Mr P. Kuris,
Mr U. Lohmus,
Mr E. Levits,
Mr J. Casadevall,

and also of Mr H. Petzold, Registrar, and Mr P. J. Mahoney, Deputy Registrar. Having deliberated in private on October 25, 1996 and March 20, 1997, delivers the following judgment, which was adopted on the last-mentioned date.

PROCEDURE

1. The case was referred to the Court on September 13, 1995 by the European Commission of Human Rights ('the Commission') within the three-month period laid down by Articles 32 § 1 and 47 of the Convention for the Protection of Human Rights and Fundamental Freedoms ('the Convention'). It originated in an application (No. 21830/93) against the United Kingdom of Great Britain and Northern Ireland lodged with the Commission under Article 25 of the Convention on May 6, 1993 by three British citizens, Mr X, Ms Y and Ms Z.

The Commission's request referred to Articles 44 and 48 of the Convention and to the declaration whereby the United Kingdom recognised the compulsory jurisdiction of the Court in accordance with Article 46. Its object was to obtain a decision on the question whether there had been a violation of Articles 8 and 14 of the Convention.

2. In response to the enquiry made pursuant to Rule 33 § 3 (d) of Rules of Court A, the applicants stated that they wished to

take part in the proceedings and designated the lawyer who would represent them (Rule 30).

3 The Chamber to be constituted included *ex officio* Sir John Freeland, the elected judge of British nationality (Article 43 of the Convention), and Mr R. Bernhardt, the Vice-President of the Court (Rule 21 § 4 (b)). On September 29, 1995, in the presence of the Registrar, the President of the Court, Mr R. Ryssdal, drew by lot the names of the other seven members, namely Mr Thór Vilhjálmsson, Mr S.K. Martens, Mr F. Bigi, Mr A.B. Baka, Mr M.A. Lopes Rocha, Mr J. Makarczyk and Mr U. Lohmus (Article 43 *in fine* of the Convention and Rule 21 § 5). Subsequently, Mr R. Macdonald and Mr N. Valticos, substitute judges, replaced Mr Bigi, who had died, and Mr Martens, who had resigned.

4. As President of the Chamber (Rule 21 § 6), Mr Bernhardt, acting through the Registrar, consulted the Agent of the United Kingdom Government ('the Government'), the applicants' representative and the Delegate of the Commission about the organization of the proceedings (Rules 37 § 1 and 38). Pursuant to the order made in consequence, the Registrar received the Government's memorial on May 2, 1996 and the applicants' memorial on May 3, 1996.

5. On May 21, 1996, the President of the Chamber granted leave to Rights International, a non-governmental human rights organization based in New York, to submit written comments (Rule 37 § 2). These were received on June 30, 1996.

6. In accordance with the decision of the President of the Chamber, the hearing took place in public in the Human Rights Building, Strasbourg, on August 27, 1996. The Court had held a preparatory meeting beforehand.

There appeared before the Court:

(a) for the Government,

Ms S. Dickson, Foreign and Commonwealth Office, Agent,
Mr D. Pannick QC,
Mr R. Singh, Counsel,
Ms H. Jenn, Department of Health,
Mr W. Jenkins, Office of Population Censuses and Surveys,
Advisers,

(b) for the Commission,

Mr J. Mucha, Delegate,

(c) for the applicants
Mr M. Penrose, Solicitor,
Mr N. Blake, Counsel.

The Court heard addresses by Mr Mucha, Mr Blake and Mr Pannick, and also replied to questions put by several of its members.

7. Following deliberations on September 2, 1996, the Chamber decided to relinquish jurisdiction forthwith in favour of a Grand Chamber (Rule 51 § 1).

8. The Grand Chamber to be constituted included *ex officio* Mr Ryssdal, President of the Court, Mr Bernhardt, Vice - President of the Court, and the other members and substitute judges (namely Mr A. Spielmann and Mr L. - E. Pettiti) of the Chamber which had relinquished jurisdiction (Rule 51 § 2 (a) and (b). On September 2, 1996, in the presence of the Registrar, the President drew by lot the names of the nine additional judges called on to complete the Grand Chamber, namely Mr F. Matscher, Mr B. Walsh, Mr C. Russo, Mr J. De Meyer, Mr I. Foighel, Mr D. Gotchev, Mr K. Jungwiert, Mr P. Kuris and Mr J. Casadevall.

9. Mr Walsh was unable to take part in the further consideration of the case and was replaced by Mr E. Levits.

10. Having taken note of the opinions of the Government's Agent, the applicants' representatives and the Commission's delegate, the Grand Chamber decided on October 25, 1996 that it was not necessary to hold a further hearing following the relinquishment of jurisdiction by the Chamber (Rule 38, taken together with Rule 51 § 6).

11. Subsequently, Mr Macdonald was unable to take part in further consideration of the case.

As to the facts

I. The Circumstances of the Case

12. The applicants are British citizens, resident in Manchester, England.

The first applicant 'X', was born in 1955 and works as a college lecturer. X is a female - to - male transsexual and will be referred to throughout this judgment using the male personal pronouns 'he', 'him' and 'his'.

Since 1979 he has lived in a permanent and stable union with the second applicant, 'Y', a woman born in 1959. The third applicant, 'Z', was born in 1992 to the second applicant as a result of artificial insemination by donor ('AID'). Y has subsequently given birth to a second child by the same method.

13. X was born with a female body. However, from the age of four he felt himself to be a sexual misfit and was drawn to 'masculine' roles of behaviour. This discrepancy caused him to suffer suicidal depression during adolescence.

In 1975, he started to take hormone treatment and to live and work as a man. In 1979, he began living with Y and later that year he underwent gender reassignment surgery, having been accepted for treatment after counselling and psychological testing.

14. In 1990, X and Y applied through their general practitioner ('GP') for AID. They were interviewed by a specialist in January 1991 with a view to obtaining treatment and their application was referred to a hospital ethics committee, supported by two references and a letter from their GP. It was, however, refused.

15. They appealed, making representations which included reference to a research study in which it was reported that in a study of 37 children raised by transsexual or homosexual parents or caretakers, there was no evidence of abnormal sexual orientation or any other adverse effect (*Sexual Identity of 37 Children Raised by Homosexual or Transsexual Parents*, R. Green, American Journal of Psychiatry, volume 135, pages 692-697, 1978).

In November 1991, the hospital ethics committee agreed to provide treatment as requested by the applicants. They asked X to acknowledge himself to be the father of the child within the meaning of the Human Fertility and Embryology Act, 1990 (see paragraph 21 below).

16. On January 30, 1992, Y was impregnated through AID treatment with sperm from an anonymous donor. X was present throughout the process. Z was born on October 13, 1992.

17. In February 1992, X had enquired of the Registrar General (see paragraph 22 below) whether there was an objection to his being registered as the father of Y's child. In a reply dated June 4, 1992 to X's Member of Parliament, the Minister of Health replied that, having taken legal advice, the Registrar General was of the

view that only a biological man could be regarded as a father for the purposes of registration. It was pointed out that the child could lawfully bear X's surname and, subject to the relevant conditions, X would be entitled to an additional personal tax allowance if he could show that he provided financial support to the child.

18. Nonetheless, following Z's birth, X and Y attempted to register the child in their joint names as mother and father. However, X was not permitted to be registered as the child's father and that part of the register was left blank. Z was given X's surname in the register (see paragraph 24 below).

19. In November 1995, X's existing job contract came to an end and he applied for approximately thirty posts. The only job offer which he received was from a university in Botswana. The conditions of service included accommodation and free education for the dependents of the employee. However, X decided not to accept the job when he was informed by a Botswanan official that only spouses and biological or adopted children would qualify as 'dependents'. He subsequently obtained another job in Manchester where he continues to work.

II. Relevant Domestic Law and Practice

A. Definition of Gender in Domestic Law

20. English law defines a person's sex by reference to biological criteria at birth and does not recognise that it can be changed by reassignment surgery (*Corbett v. Corbett* [1971] Probate *Reports p. 83* and *R v. Tan* [1983] Queen's Bench Reports p. 1053 (Courts of Appeal)).

As a result of this principle, a female-to-male transsexual is not permitted to marry a woman and cannot be regarded as the father of a child.

B. Children Conceived by Artificial Insemination

21. The Human Fertility and Embryology Act 1990 ('the 1990 Act') provides, *inter alia,* that where an unmarried woman gives birth as a result of AID with the involvement of her male partner, the latter, rather than the donor of the sperm, shall be treated for legal purposes as the father of the child (Section 28(3)).

C. Registration of Births

22. Section 1(1) of the Births and Deaths Registration Act 1953 ('the 1953 Act') requires that certain prescribed details concerning the birth of every child born in England and Wales, including the names of the parents, be entered in a register. The Registrar General is the official ultimately responsible for the administration of this scheme.

23. If the child's father (or the person regarded by law as the father: see paragraph 21 above) is not married to the mother, his name shall not automatically be entered on the register in the space provided for the father. However, it will be entered if he and the mother jointly request that this be done (Section 10 of the 1953 Act, as amended by the Family Law Reform Act, 1987).

24. A birth certificate takes the form either of an authenticated copy of the entry in the register of births or an extract from it. A certificate of the latter kind, known as a 'short certificate of birth', is in a prescribed form and contains such particulars as are prescribed by regulations made under the 1953 Act. These particulars are the name, surname, sex and date and place of birth of the individual concerned. Under English law, a child may be given any first name or surname as the parents see fit, and may change his or her name or surname at any time, without restriction.

D. Parental Responsibility

25. 'Parental responsibility' in respect of a child automatically vests in the mother and, where she is married, in her husband. It may, additionally, be granted to certain other persons (see paragraphs 26 - 27) below.

'Parental responsibility' means all the rights, duties, powers, responsibility and authority which by law a parent of a child has in relation to the child and his or her property (Section 3 of the Children Act, 1989; 'the 1989 Act').

It does not, without more, confer on the child any rights in the property of the person granted parental responsibility, such as the right to inherit on intestacy or to financial support. Similarly, it does not entitle the child to benefit through that person from the transmission of tenancies pursuant to certain statutory provisions, from nationality and immigration measures or from rights accruing from that person's citizenship in the European Union.

26. The father of a child who was not married to the mother at the time of the birth may apply for a court order granting him parental responsibility or may attain it by virtue of an agreement, in a prescribed form, with the mother (Section 4 of the 1989 Act).

27. Parental responsibility cannot vest in any other person, unless a 'residence order' in respect of the child is made in his or her favour.

A residence order is 'an order settling the arrangements to be made as to the person with whom the child is to live' (Section 8 of the 1989 Act). Any person may apply for such an order (although individuals outside certain defined categories must first seek the leave of the court in order to apply).

Where the court makes a residence order in respect of any person who is not the parent or guardian of the child, that person is automatically vested with parental responsibility for the child as long as the residence order remains in force (Section 12(2) of the 1989 Act).

28. Thus, although the first applicant could not apply directly for parental responsibility of the third applicant, he could apply with the second applicant for a joint residence order which would have the effect of giving him parental responsibility while it remained in force. On June 24, 1994, Mr Justice Douglas - Brown in the Manchester High Court made a joint residence order in favour of two cohabiting lesbian women in respect of the child of one of them (unreported).

Proceedings before the Commission

29. In their application to the Commission of May 6, 1993 (no. 21830/93) as declared admissible, the applicants complained that, contrary to Article 8 of the Convention, they were denied respect for their family and private life as a result of the lack of recognition of the first applicant's role as father to the third applicant and that the resulting situation in which they were placed was discriminatory, in violation of Articles 8 and 14.

30. On December 1, 1994, the Commission declared admissible the complaints under Article 8 and 14 of the Convention, and declared inadmissible complaints under Articles

12 and 13. In its report of June 27, 1995 (Article 31), it expressed the opinions that there had been a violation of Article 8 of the Convention (thirteen votes to five) and that it was not necessary to examine whether there had been a violation of Article 14 in conjunction with Article 8 (seventeen votes to one). The full text of the Commission's opinion and of the five separate opinions contained in its report are reproduced as an annexe to this judgment[fn3].

Final Submissions Made to the Court

31. At the hearing on August 27, 1996 the Government, as they had done in their memorial, asked the Court to hold that there had been no violation of Article 8 or 14 of the Convention.

On the same occasion, the applicants requested the Court to reach a finding of violation and to award just satisfaction under Article 50.

AS TO THE LAW

I. ALLEGED VIOLATION OF ARTICLE 8 OF THE CONVENTION

32. The applicants, with whom the Commission agreed, submitted that the lack of legal recognition of the relationship between X and Z amounted to a violation of Article 8 of the Convention, which provides:

1. Everyone has the right to respect for his private and family life, his home and his correspondence.
2. There shall be no interference by a public authority with the exercise of this right except such as is in accordance with the law and is necessary in a democratic society in the interests of national security, public safety or the economic well-being of the country, for the prevention of disorder or crime, for the protection of health or morals, or for the protection of the rights and freedoms of others.

The Government denied that Article 8 was applicable and, in the alternative, claimed that there had been no violation.

A. The existence of 'family life'

33. The applicants submitted that they had shared a 'family life' with the meaning of Article 8 since Z's birth. They emphasised that, according to the jurisprudence of the Commission and the Court, social reality, rather than formal legal status, was decisive. Thus, it was important to note that X had irrevocably changed many of his physical characteristics and provided financial and emotional support to Y and Z. To all appearances, the applicants lived as a traditional family.

34. The Government did not accept that the concept of 'family life' applied to the relationships between X and Y or X and Z. They reasoned that X and Y had to be treated as two woman living together, because X was still regarded as female under domestic law and a complete change of sex was not medically possible. Case-law of the Commission indicated that a 'family' could not be based on two unrelated persons of the same sex, including a lesbian couple (see the Commission's decisions on admissibility in X. and Y. versus the United Kingdom, application no. 9369/81, Decisions and Reports vol. 32, p. 220 and Kerkhoven versus the Netherlands, application no. 15666/89). Nor could X be said to enjoy 'family life' with Z since he was not related to the child by blood, marriage or adoption.

At the hearing before the Court, Counsel for the Government accepted that if X and Y applied for and were granted a joint residence order in respect of Z (see paragraph 27 above), it would be difficult to maintain that there was no 'family life' for the purposes of Article 8.

35. The Commission considered that the relationship between X and Y could not be equated with that of a lesbian couple, since X was living in society as a man, having undergone gender reassignment surgery. Aside from the fact the X was registered at birth as a woman and was therefore under a legal incapacity to marry Y or be registered as Z's father, the applicants' situation was indistinguishable from the tradition notion of 'family life'.

36. The Court recalls that the notion of 'family life' in Article 8 is not confined solely to families based on marriage and may encompass other *de facto* relationships (see the Marckx versus Belgium judgment of June 13, 1979, Series A no. 31, pp. 14, § 31, the

Keegan versus Ireland judgment of May 26, 1994, Series A no. 290, pp. 17, § 44 and the Kroon and Others versus The Netherlands judgment of October 27, 1994, Series A no. 297 - C, pp. 55 - 56, § 30). When deciding whether a relationship can be said to amount to 'family life', a number of factors may be relevant, including whether the couple live together, the length of their relationship and whether they have demonstrated their commitment to each other by having children together or by any other means (see, for example, the above - mentioned Kroon and Others judgment, loc. cit.).

37. In the present case, the Court notes that X is a transsexual who has undergone gender reassignment surgery. He has lived with Y, to all appearances as her male partner, since 1979. The couple applied jointly for, and were granted, treatment by AID to allow Y to have a child. X was involved throughout that process and has acted as Z's 'father' in every respect since the birth (see paragraphs 14-16 above). In these circumstances, the Court considers that *de facto* family ties link the three applicants.

It follows that Article 8 is applicable.

B. Compliance with Article 8

1. The arguments as to the applicable general principles

38. The applicants pointed out that the Court had recognised in its Rees v. the United Kingdom judgment (October 17, 1986, Series A no. 106, pp. 19, § 47, that the need for appropriate legal measures affecting transsexuals should be kept under review having regard in particular to scientific and societal developments. They maintained that there had been significant development since that decision: in particular, the European Parliament and the Parliamentary Assembly of the Council of Europe had called for comprehensive recognition of transsexual identity (Resolution OJ 1989 C256 and Recommendation 1117 September 29, 1989 respectively); the European Court of Justice had decided that the dismissal of a transsexual for a reason related to gender reassignment amounted to discrimination contrary to Community Directive 76/207 (P. v. S. and Cornwall County Council, C - 13/94, April 30, 1996); and scientific research had been published which suggested that transsexuality was not merely a psychological disorder, but had a physiological basis in

the structure of the brain (see, for example, *Biological Aspects of Transsexualism*, Professor L. J. G. Gooren, Council of Europe document no CJ - DE/XXIII (93) 5 and *A Sex Difference in the Human Brain and its Relation to Transsexuality*, Zhou, Hofman, Gooren and Swaab, *Nature* vol. 378, p. 68, November 2, 1995). These developments made it appropriate for the Court to re-examine the principles underlying its decisions in the above-mentioned Rees case and Cossey v. the United Kingdom (September 27, 1990, Series A no. 184), in so far as they had an impact on the present problem. The Court should now hold that the notion or respect for family and/or private life required States to recognise the present sexual identity of post-operative transsexuals for legal purposes, including parental rights.

However, they also emphasised that the issue in their case was very different from that in Rees and Cossey, since X was not seeking to amend his own birth certificate but rather to be named in Z's birth certificate as her father. They submitted that the margin of appreciation afforded to the respondent State should be narrower in such a case and the need for positive action to ensure respect much stronger, having regard to the interests of the child in having her social father recognised as such by law.

39. The Government contended that Contracting States enjoyed a wide margin of appreciation in relation to the complex issues raised by transsexuality, in view of the lack of a uniform approach to the problem and the transitional state of the law. They denied that there had been any significant change in the scientific or legal position with regard to transsexuals. Despite recent research, there still remained uncertainty as to the essential nature of the condition and there was not yet any sufficiently broad consensus between the member States of the Council of Europe (see, for example, *the Report of the Proceedings of the XXIIIrd Colloquy on European Law, Transsexualism, Medicine and the Law*, Council of Europe, 1993 and *Another Important Organ*, S. M. Breedlove, *Nature* vol 378, p. 15, November 2, 1995). The judgment of the European Court of Justice in P. v. S. and Cornwall County Council (cited in paragraph 38 above) did not assist the applicants because it was not concerned with the extent to which a State was obliged to recognise a person's change of sex for legal purposes.

Like the applicants, they stressed that the present case was not merely concerned with transsexuality. Since it also raised difficult and novel questions relating to the treatment of children born by AID, the State should enjoy a very broad margin of appreciation.

40. The Commission referred to a clear trend within the Contracting States towards the legal recognition of gender reassignment. It took the view that, in the case of a transsexual who had undergone reassignment surgery in the Contracting State and who lived there as part of a family relationship, there had to be a presumption in favour of legal recognition of that relationship, the denial of which required special justification.

2. The Court's General Approach

41. The Court reiterates that, although the essential object of Article 8 is to protect the individual against arbitrary interferences by the public authorities, there may in additon be positive obligations inherent in an effective respect for private or family life. The boundaries between the State's positive and negative obligations under this provision do not always lend themselves to precise definition; nonetheless, the applicable principles are similar. In both contexts, regard must be had to the fair balance that has to be struck between the competing interests of the individual and of the community as a whole, and in both cases the State enjoys a certain margin of appreciation (see, for example, the above-mentioned Rees judgment, pp. 14, § 35 and the above-mentioned Kroon and Others judgment, pp. 56, § 31).

42. The present case is distinguishable from the previous cases concerning transsexuals which have been brought before the Court (see the above-mentioned Rees judgment, the above-mentioned Cossey judgment and the B. v. France judgment of March 25, 1992, Series A no. 232 - C), because here the applicants' complaint is not that the domestic law makes no provision for the recognition of the transsexual's change of identity, but rather that it is not possible for such a person to be registered as the father of a child; indeed, it is for this reason that the Court is examining this case in relation to family, rather than private life (see paragraph 37 above).

43. It is true that the Court has held in the past that where the existence of a family tie with a child has been established, the State must act in a manner calculated to enable that tie to be developed and legal safeguards must be established that render possible, from the moment of birth or as soon as practicable thereafter, the child's integration in his family (see for example the above-mentioned Marckx judgment; the Johnston and Others v. Ireland judgment of December 18, 1986, Series A no 112, pp. 29, § 72; the above-mentioned Keegan judgment; and the above-mentioned Kroon and Others judgment, pp. 56, § 32). However, hitherto in this context it has been called upon to consider only family ties existing between biological parents and their offspring. The present case raises different issues, since Z was conceived by AID and is not related, in the biological sense, to X who is a transsexual.

44. The Court observes that there is no common European standard with regard to the granting of parental rights to transsexuals. In addition, it has not been established before the Court that there exists any generally shared approach amongst the High Contracting Parties with regard to the manner in which the social relationship between a child conceived by AID and the person who performs the role of father should be reflected in law. Indeed, according to the information available to the Court, although the technology of medically assisted procreation has been available in Europe for several decades, many of the issues to which it gives rise, particularly with regard to the question of filiation, remain the subject of debate. For example, there is no consensus amongst the member States of the Council of Europe on the question whether the interests of a child conceived in such a way are best served by preserving the anonymity of the donor of the sperm or whether the child should have the right to know the donor's identity.

Since the issues in the case, therefore, touch on areas where there is little common ground amongst the member States of the Council of Europe and, generally speaking, the law appears to be in a transitional stage, the respondent State must be afforded a wise margin of appreciation (see *mutatis mutandis* the above mentioned Rees judgment, pp. 15, § 37 and the above-mentioned Cossey judgment, pp. 16, § 40).

3. Whether a fair balance was struck in the instant case

45. The applicants, with whom the Commission agreed, argued that a number of consequences flowed from the lack of legal recognition of X's role as father. Perhaps most importantly, the child's sense of security within the family might be undermined. Furthermore, the absence of X's name on her birth certificate might cause distress on those occasions when a full-length certificate had to be produced, for example on registration with a doctor or school, if an insurance policy was taken out on her life or when she applied for a passport. Although Z was a British citizen by birth and could trace connection through her mother in immigration and nationality matters, problems could still arise if X sought to work abroad. For example, he had already had to turn down an offer of employment in Botswana because he had been informed that Y and Z would not have been recognised as his 'dependents' and would not, therefore, have been entitled to receive certain benefits (see paragraph 19 above). Moreover, in contrast to the position where a parent-child relationship was recognised by law, Z could not inherit from X on intestacy or succeed to certain tenancies on X's death. The possibility of X obtaining a residence order in respect of Z (see paragraph 27 above) did not satisfy the requirement of respect, since this would entail the incurring of legal expense and an investigation by a court welfare officer which might distress the child.

In their submission, it was apparent that the legal recognition sought would not interfere with the rights of others or require any fundamental reorganisation of the United Kingdom system of registration of births, since the Human Fertility and Embryology Act 1990 allowed a man who was not a transsexual to be registered as the father of a child born to his female partner by AID (see paragraph 21 above).

46. The Government pointed out that the applicants were not restrained in any way from living together as a 'family' and they asserted that the concerns expressed by them were highly theoretical. Furthermore, X and Y could jointly apply for a residence order, conferring on them parental rights and duties in relation to Z (see paragraph 27 above).

47. First, the Court observes that the community as a whole has an interest in maintaining a coherent system of family law

which places the best interests of the child at the forefront. In this respect, the Court notes that, whilst it has not been suggested that the amendment to the law sought by the applicants would be harmful to the interests of Z or of children conceived by AID in general, it is not clear that it would necessarily be to the advantage of such children.

In these circumstances, the Court considers that the State may justifiably be cautious in changing the law, since it is possible that the amendment sought might have undesirable or unforeseen ramifications for children in Z's position. Furthermore, such an amendment might have implications in other areas of family law. For example, the law might be open to criticism on the ground of inconsistency if a female-to-male transsexual were granted the possibility of becoming a 'father' in law while still being treated for other legal purposes as female and capable of contracting marriage to a man.

48. Against these general interests, the Court must weigh the disadvantages suffered by the applicants as a result of the refusal to recognise X in law as Z's 'father'.

The applicants identify a number of legal consequences flowing from this lack of recognition (see paragraph 45 above). For example, they point to the fact that if X were to die intestate, Z would have no automatic right of inheritance. The Court notes, however, that the problem could be solved in practice if X were to make a will. No evidence has been adduced to show that X is the beneficiary of any transmissible tenancies of the type referred to; similarly, since Z is a British citizen by birth and can trace connection through her mother in immigration and nationality matters, she will not be disadvantaged in this respect by the lack of a legal relationship with X.

The Court considers, therefore, that these legal consequences would be unlikely to cause undue hardship given the facts of the present case.

49. In addition, the applicants claimed that Z might suffer various social or developmental difficulties. Thus, it was argued that she would be caused distress on those occasions when it was necessary to produce her birth certificate.

In relation to the absence of X's name on the birth certificate, the Court notes, first, that unless X and Y choose to make such information public, neither the child nor any third party will know that this absence is a consequence of the fact that X was born female. It follows that the applicants are in a similar position to any other family where, for whatever reason, the person who performs the role of the child's 'father' is not registered as such. The Court does not find it established that any particular stigma still attaches to children or families in such circumstances.

Secondly, the Court recalls that in the United Kingdom a birth certificate is not in common use for administrative or identification purposes and that there are few occasions when it is necessary to produce a full-length certificate (see paragraph 24 above).

50. The applicants were also concerned, more generally, that Z's sense of personal identity and security within her family would be affected by the lack of legal recognition of X as father.

In this respect, the Court notes that X is not prevented in any way from acting as Z's father in the social sense. Thus, for example, he lives with her, providing emotional and financial support to her and Y, and he is free to describe himself to her and others as her 'father' and to give her his surname (see paragraph 24 above). Furthermore, together with Y, he could apply for a joint residence order in respect of Z, which would automatically confer on them full parental responsibility for her in English law (see paragraph 27 above).

51. It is impossible to predict the extent to which the absence of a legal connection between X and Z will affect the latter's development. As previously mentioned, at the present time there is uncertainty with regard to how the interests of children in Z's position can best be protected (see paragraph 44 above) and the Court should not adopt or impose any single viewpoint.

52. In conclusion, given that transsexuality raise complex scientific, legal, moral and social issues, in respect of which there is no generally shared approach among the Contracting States, the Court is of the opinion that Article 8 cannot, in this context, be taken to imply an obligation for the respondent State formally to recognise as the father of a child a person who is not the biological father. That being so, the fact that the law of the United Kingdom does not allow special legal recognition of the

relationship between X and Z does not amount to a failure to respect family life within the meaning of that provision.

It follows that there has been no violation of Article 8 of the Convention.

II. ALLEGED VIOLATION OF ARTICLE 14 OF THE CONVENTION TAKEN IN CONJUNCTION WITH ARTICLE 8

53. In addition, the applicants complained of discrimination contrary to Article 14 of the Convention, which provides:

> The enjoyment of the rights and freedom set forth in [the] Convention shall be secured without discrimination on any ground such as sex, race, colour, language, religion, political or other opinion, national or social origin, association with a national minority, property, birth or other status.

54. The applicants did not develop this complaint in their memorial, since they adopted the findings of the Commission (see paragraph 55 below). However, at the hearing before the Court, their Counsel referred in particular to the fact that had X been born a man he could have been registered as Z's father under the provisions of the Human Fertility and Embryology Act 1990 (see paragraph 21 above).

55. The Government submitted that no separate issue arose in connection with Article 14. In view of its finding of a violation of Article 8 of the Convention, the Commission did not find it necessary to examine this complaint.

56. The Court considers that the complaint under Article 14 is tantamount to a restatement of the complaint under Article 8, and raises no separate issue. In view of its finding in respect of the latter provision (see paragraph 52 above), there is no need to examine the issue again in the context of Article 14.

Accordingly, it is not necessary to consider this complaint.

For these reasons the court

1. *Holds* unanimously that Article 8 of the Convention is applicable in the present case;
2. *Holds* by fourteen votes to six that there has been no violation of Article 8;

3. *Holds* by seventeen votes to three that it is not necessary to consider the complaint under Article 14 of the Convention taken in conjunction with Article 8.

Done in English and French and delivered at a public hearing at the Human Rights Building, Strasbourg, on April 22, 1997.

Rolv Ryssdal
President

Herbert Petzold
Registrar

In accordance with Article 51 § 1 of the Convention and Rule 53 § 2 of Rules of Court A, the following separate opinions are annexed to this judgment:

(a) concurring opinion of Mr Pettiti;
(b) concurring opinion of Mr De Meyer;
(c) partly dissenting opinion of Mr Casadevall joined by Mr Russo and Mr Makarcyzk;
(d) dissenting opinion of Mr Thór Vilhjálmsson;
(e) dissenting opinion of Mr Foighel;
(f) dissenting opinion of Mr Gotchev.

R. R.
H. P.

CONCURRING OPINION OF JUDGE PETTITI

(Provisional Translation)

I voted with the majority for the finding that there was no violation of Article 8 of the Convention. However, I consider that the impact of the judgment could have been strengthened by expanding the reasoning and adopting different wording in a number of places.

The text adopted seems to me to be based too much on the personal demands of X and Y alone, which are specific to their individual situations, and on a weighing of the practical and social advantages and disadvantages which might result from changing, or not changing, Z's civil status. As this is the first case in which the European Court has had to deal with both transsexualism and the problem of a child's right to know his biological origins, it should, in my opinion, have given more thought to the assessment of family life within the meaning of Article 8 and to the conflict of interests between parents and children.

Moreover, the instant case concerned a couple, X and Y, composed of post-operative transsexual and a woman who had produced the child Z as a result of artificial insemination by an anonymous donor.

Did X, Y and Z form a family? A family, in general, cannot be a mere aggregate of the individuals living under one roof. The ethical and social dimension of a family cannot be ignored or underestimated. If there was a family, as there appears to have been in the case before the Court, can the object sought by X be imposed on Z?

Studies have shown that not all transsexuals have the same aptitude for family life (after an authorised operation) as a non-transsexual (see the joint research by Alby *et al.*, International Freudian Association, 'Sexual identity and transsexuals', and the study by L. Pettiti, 'Les transsexuals, Que sais - je?', Presses Universitaires de France).

The X, Y and Z case touched upon the conflict between the demand of a female-to-male transsexual (X) to be registered as the father of his female cohabitee's child and the demand which could in due course be made by Z, who might sooner or later come to consider that her own interest lies in finding out who her biological father was. The Court should therefore also have assessed the conflict between family law, the law of filiation and the direct effect of the United Nations Convention on the Rights of the Child, to which it did not refer.

Should there be another case like this one, it would no doubt be desirable for the Commission and the Court to suggest to the parties that a lawyer be instructed specifically to represent the interests of the child alone.

The growing number of precarious and unstable family situations is creating new difficulties for children of first and second families, whether legitimate, natural, successive or superimposed, and will in the future call for thoughtful consideration of the identity of the family and the meaning of family life which Article 8 is intended to protect, taking into account the fact that priority must be given to the interests of the child and its future. In the particular case of X, Y and Z, the consequences of finding a violation could already be gauged, namely the ambivalent situation which could result from a female-to-male transsexual being registered as a father while being considered under British law to be of female sex and registered as such in the register of births, marriages and deaths (see paragraph 47 of the judgment).

In the Cossey v. the United Kingdom and B. v. France cases, the Court, and its judges in their separate opinions, emphasised the civil-law problems raised by transsexualism and the knock-on effects of a change of civil status on the right to marriage, divorce, the law of succession, the law of adoption, etc.

The Court's conclusions (see paragraphs 47, 51 and 52 of the present judgment) were therefore justified and prudent, but could in my opinion have been supplemented by a legal, sociological and ethical examination of the whole problem and the diversity of the rights and values to be attributed to each of the persons who go to make up a family.

CONCURRING OPINION OF JUDGE DE MEYER

I. Applicability of Article 8

I would observe that, as far as X is concerned, this case should have been dealt with from the point of view of private, rather than family life.

There is certainly family life between Y and Z. However, between X and the two other applicants there is only the 'appearances' of 'family ties' [fn4], which, of course, concern the private life of the three applicants.

II. Compliance with Article 8

There was no reason to refer, once again, to a so-called 'margin of appreciation' enjoyed by the State[fn5]. It was enough to recognise that in not allowing X to be registered as Z's father, the respondent State had not 'acted arbitrarily or unreasonably or failed to strike a fair balance between the respective interests' involved[fn6].

There was also no need to consider that, on the issues at stake, there is no 'common European standard' or no 'common ground', 'generally shared approach', or 'consensus amongst the members States of the Council of Europe', or that these issues 'remain the subject of debate', or member States of the Council of Europe', or that these issues 'remain the subject of debate', or that the law of member States concerning them 'appears to be in a transitional stage'[fn7]. Nor was it helpful to remark that something 'is impossible to predict', or that 'there is uncertainty with regard to' a certain question [fn8]. Nothing of that kind was relevant. All we had to do was to identify the principles which, in our view, had to be applied and the rules to be observed.

These principles and rules are quite simple. Indeed, it is self-evident that a person who is manifestly not the father of a child has no right to be recognised as her father.

PARTLY DISSENTING OPINION OF JUDGE CASADEVALL JOINED BY JUDGES RUSSO AND MAKARCZYK

(Provisional Translation)

1. The majority did not see fit to depart from the Court's existing case-law, in particular the Rees and Cossey judgments (notwithstanding the B.v. France judgment). Although the underlying problem remains the same (sexual dysphoria and sex changes), I consider that the present case has important distinguishing features which could justify a decision that there has been a violation of Article 8 taken separately without that decision entailing a complete reversal of the Court's case-law.

2. The subject is certainly a sensitive one and it raises numerous moral and ethical problems. But it is no less certain that more and more States (at present nearly half the members of the Council of Europe) are taking steps to adapt and harmonise their legislation with a view to full legal recognition of the new identity of those who have had sex change operations (in accordance with the relevant regulations and under the supervision of medical and ethical committees) so as to alleviate, as far as possible, the distress some human beings are suffering (see the resolution adopted by

the European Parliament on September 12, 1989 and the Recommendation of the Parliamentary Assembly of the Council of Europe of September 29, 1989).

3. Equally certainly, every State has a legitimate right to regulate such matters according to the aspirations of its people and its legal system, and in doing so has a 'margin of appreciation' which varies from field to field. That means that it must not go beyond the limits imposed by respect for the fundamental rights guaranteed by the Convention.

4. The considerations set out in Judge Martens' dissenting opinion in the Cossey case remain wholly applicable to the present case. When a person has undergone gruelling medical treatment, hormone therapy and dangerous surgery, and when his physiological sex has been brought into harmony, as far as possible, with his psychological sex, it is right and proper for his new identity to be recognised not only by society but also in law; "... refusal [of such recognition] can only be qualified as cruel".

5. I think the present case is more complex than the earlier Rees and Cossey cases (i) because it concerns three people, (ii) because it is as much about private life as family life for the purposes of Article 8, and (iii) having regard to the following facts.

(a) After suffering since childhood from sexual dysphoria X underwent hormone therapy in 1975 and began to live and work as a man (see paragraph 13 of the judgment).

(b) Four years later he began to live with a woman, Y, and was then after going through the required procedure and undergoing psychological test, given permission to have sex change operation. According to the applicants, the operation was financed by the United Kingdom National Health Service.

(c) After an initial refusal and appeal the hospital ethics committee gave the go-ahead and X and Y were given permission for treatment with a view to artificial insemination by anonymous donor (see paragraph 15 of the judgment).

(d) Previously, X had been asked to make an acknowledgment of paternity pursuant to Section 28(3) of the Human Fertility and Embryology Act 1990, which provides:

"where a man, who is not married to the mother, is party to the treatment which results in the sperm being placed in the woman, he shall be deemed to be the father of the child".

(e) X gave his agreement and his support. Y was impregnated and Z was born in 1992; Z has lived since then with X and Y, who act as her parents (see paragraphs 16-19 of the judgment).

(f) In reply to the registration request, the Minister of Health informed X that only a biological male could be regarded as the father for the purposes of registration (see paragraph 17 of the judgment).

6. I accordingly summarise the problem in two essential points, on which I base my opinion.

The first concerns the concept of 'family life'. It seems to me undeniable that the relationship which binds the three applicants together, in their own experience and as perceived by society (Y is Z's mother and X publicly assumes the roles of male partner and father), permits the finding that they enjoy real family life, which, according to the Court, "... is not confined solely to marriage-based relationships and may encompass other *de facto* 'family' ties where the parties are living together outside of marriage" (see the Keegan v. Ireland judgment of May 26, 1994, Series A no. 290, pp. 17, § 44).

It should be noted that when, at the hearing, Judge Makarczyk asked Mr Pannick, the Government's Counsel, if the Government would have changed it position on the question of family life if the applicants had requested and obtained a joint residence order, he was given the following answer: "... it would be very difficult indeed for the United Kingdom then to submit to this Court that there is no family life for the purposes of Article 8" (see the verbatim record of the hearing, p. 30).

The second point-having regard to the facts of the case and the principle of legal certainty and even foreseeability-is that since the State permitted X to undergo hormone treatment and then, after he had gone through the required procedure and undergone psychological tests, permitted and even financed irreversible surgery, issued documents mentioning his new sexual identity and authorised Y (after an acknowledgment of paternity prescribed by law had been obtained from X) to undergo artificial insemination which led to the birth of Z and a second child since, it must accept the consequences and take all the measures needed to enable the applicants to live normal lives, without discriminations, under their new identity and with respect for their right to private and family life.

7. For these reasons, I conclude that there has been a violation of Article 8 of the Convention.

Dissenting opinion of judge Thór Vilhjálmsson

Article 8 is applicable in this case. On this point I share the opinion of the Court which is set out in the judgment.

As stated in paragraph 21 of the judgment, 'the 1990 Act' provides that in the United Kingdom the male partner of a woman who gives birth to a child as a result of AID shall be treated for legal purposes as the father of the child. This rule was not applied in the present case because the partner of the mother is a female-to-male transsexual. Had X been born a man, he would have been registered as the father of the child Z.

The case at hand differs from the Cossey case and the Rees case, and for me it is an important difference that the State is not in this case requested to change entries in the register that were correct when they were made. Under UK law it is now possible for the register to contain statements that are not in conformity with biological facts but are based on legal considerations (see paragraph 21 above). For this reason I have not found it difficult to come to the conclusion that X had, under Article 8 of the Convention, a right to be registered as the father of Z. This was not accepted in the UK. I am of the opinion that this showed lack of respect for the applicants' family life. This is, I find, just as true in respect of Z as of X and Y. In a country where it is laid down by legislation that the partner of a mother who gives birth to a child as a result of AID can be registered as the father, it is obviously accepted that the family ties between all concerned are of importance. I fail to see why this should be otherwise in the case before the Court, where the partner is a transsexual. Accordingly, I have come to the conclusion that there has been a violation of Article 8.

As already stated, X was not in the same position as other partners who had the right to be registered as fathers. This is in my opinion discrimination on the ground of sex. Accordingly, I find that there was a violation of Article 14 taken in conjunction with Article 8.

DISSENTING OPINION OF JUDGE FOIGHEL

1. Article 8 expressly states that "Everyone has the right to respect for his private and family life ..." (emphasis added). In my view this includes transsexuals.

2. As in the Cossey case, I find that a government's failure to ensure that full legal recognition is given to a transsexual's change of sex following successful gender reassignment surgery amounts to a violation of Article 8 of the Convention.

3. In our joint dissenting opinion in the Cossey case, Judges Palm, Pekkanen and I referred to the view expressed in earlier judgments, that 'the law appears to be in a transitional state' and that 'the need for appropriate legal measures should be kept under review having regard particularly to scientific and societal developments'.

This important and relevant statement underlines the fact that, with regard to the status of transsexuals, legal solutions must necessarily follow medical, social and moral developments.

4. While the present complaint differs in some aspects from the earlier cases involving transsexuals, it is a fact that X, like Cossey, Rees and many other individuals, is convinced that he does not truly belong to the sex the biological characteristics which he had at birth. The central issue here is that the law should fully take account of his gender reassignment. This is not primarily a case concerning the welfare of a child; instead, it is about the respect to be afforded to a transsexual taking part in family life.

I cannot therefore accept the majority's argument in paragraphs 47 and 51 that the recognition of X as father could be harmful to the child, especially since it is stated in paragraph 47 that it is 'not clear' whether this recognition would be to the advantage of the child or would be harmful to her.

5. Paragraph 38 lists the most recent developments in the field of recognition of transsexuality. These changes underline the point made seven years ago in the above-mentioned joint dissenting opinion, that '(t)here is a growing awareness of the importance of each person's own identity and of the need to tolerate and accept the differences between individual human beings. Furthermore, the right to privacy and the right to live, as far as possible, one's own life undisturbed are increasingly accepted'. These developments are not reflected in the view of the majority.

6. It is part of our common European heritage that governments are under a duty to take special care of individuals who are disadvantaged in any way. That the United Kingdom Government to a certain extent share this view is demonstrated by the fact that the State made it possible for X to undergo the surgery which brought his physiology into conformity with his psychology. Similarly, the authorities agreed to allow X and Y to have a child through AID. Furthermore, the couple could probably obtain a joint residence order in respect of the child which would further normalise their family life.

I am of course aware that in some countries and some circles there exist negative attitudes towards transsexuals, based on deeply rooted moral and ethical notions. However, such attitudes seem slowly to be changing in European societies. As I have mentioned, the Government did not demonstrate such attitudes at the time of X's operation or when X and Y were granted permission to undergo AID treatment.

7. It is the Court's task to balance the rights of the individual against the interests of society as a whole. However, the Government have not adduced any convincing arguments with regard to these competing interests. Moreover, they have made no attempt to justify their failure to help X further by ensuring that his change of sex receives legal recognition, recognition which would benefit him and harm no one.

8. I find Article 8 violated in this case.

9. The Human Fertility and Embryology Act 1990 provides

that where an unmarried woman gives birth as a result of AID with the involvement of her male partner, the latter, rather than the donor of the sperm, shall be treated for legal purposes as the father of the child (Section 28(3): see paragraph 21 above). According to the Registration Act 1953, the child's father (or the person regarded by law as the father) can have his name entered in the register if he and the mother jointly request that this be done (Section 10 of the 1953 Act, as amended by the Family Law Reform Act 1987: see paragraph 23 above). Had the present applicant been a biological man from birth, albeit not the biological father of the child, this rule would certainly have been applied. X, however, because he was a transsexual, was denied this right.

10. Article 14 says '...without discrimination on any ground such as sex, race, colour ... birth or other status'. These characteristics are all 'nature-given'. A transsexual is someone who has been born different from others, someone who has been born with a 'defect'. The British law puts transsexuals in a special category and discriminates against them.

This, I find, is a clear violation of Article 14 taken in conjunction with Article 8.

DISSENTING OPINION OF JUDGE GOTCHEV

To my regret, I cannot agree with the majority in the present case, for the following reasons.

I agree that, according to the constant case-law of the Court, the relationships between X, Y and Z can be regarded as 'family life' (see paragraph 37 of the judgment). Since it was established that *de facto* family ties of the kind protected by Article 8 of the Convention existed between the applicants, I consider that the State was under a duty to act in a manner calculated to enable those ties to be developed and to establish legal safeguards to render possible, from the moment of birth or as soon as practicable thereafter, the child's integration into the family (see the case-law cited in paragraph 43 of the judgment). In my view, this obligation entails the possibility for X to be recognised in law as Z's father.

It is true that there is no common standard among the Contracting States with regard to the parental rights of transsexuals and I agree with the conclusion that States must therefore be allowed a wide margin of appreciation in this area (see paragraph 44 of the judgment). It is nonetheless necessary for the Court to establish whether the present situation under British law, whereby the transsexual 'father' of a child conceived by AID was denied the possibility to be recognised as such in law, struck a fair balance between the individuals' rights to respect for family life and any countervailing general interest. In striking this balance, the welfare of the child should be the prevailing consideration, irrespective of the manner of his or her conception or the transsexuality of the 'social father'.

For these reasons, I find violations of Articles 8 and 14 of the Convention.

FOOTNOTES

1. The case is numbered 75/1995/581/667. The first number is the case's position on the list of cases referred to the Court in the relevant year (second number). The last two numbers indicates the case's position on the list of cases referred to the Court since its creation and on the list of the corresponding originating applications to the Commission. *(Back to FN1)*
2. Rules A apply to all cases referred to the Court before the entry into force of Protocol No. 9 (October 1, 1994) and thereafter only to cases concerning States not bound by that Protocol. They correspond to the Rules that came into force on January 1, 1983, as amended several times subsequently, *(Back to FN2)*
3. Note by the Registrar. For practical reasons this annexe will appear only with the printed version of the judgment (in Reports of Judgments and Decisions - 1996), but copies of the Commission's report are obtainable from the registry. *(Back to FN3)*
4. Paragraphs 33 and 37 of this judgment. *(Back to FN4)*
5. Paragraphs 41 and 44 of this judgment. See also Section III of my opinion in the recent case of Z v. Finland, judgment of February 25, 1997. *(Back of FN5)*
6. Velosa Barreto v. Portugal judgment of November 21, 1995, Series A no. 334, pp. 12, § 30. *(Back to FN6)*
7. Paragraphs 44 and 52 of this judgment. *(Back to FN7)*
8. Paragraph 51 of this judgment. *(Back to FN8)*

EUROPEAN COURT OF HUMAN RIGHTS

In the Dudgeon case:

The European Court of Human Rights, taking its decision in plenary session in application of Rule 48 of the Rules of Court and composed of the following judges:

Mr R. Ryssdal, President,
Mr M. Zekia,
Mr J. Cremona,
Mr Thór Vilhjálmsson,
Mr W. Ganshof Van Der Meersch,
Mrs. D. Bindschedler - Robert,
Mr D. Evrigenis,
Mr G. Lagergren,
Mr L. Liesch,
Mr F. Golcuklu,
Mr F. Matscher,
Mr J. Pinheiro Farinha,
Mr E. Garcia De Enterria,
Mr L. -E. Pettiti,
Mr B. Walsh,
Sir Vincent Evans,
Mr R. Macdonald,
Mr C. Russo,
Mr R. Bernhardt,

and also Mr M.A. Eissen, Registrar, and Mr H. Petzold, Deputy Registrar.

Having deliberated in private on April 24 and 25 and from September 21 to 23, 1981, delivers the following judgment, which was adopted on the last - mentioned date.

Procedure

1. The Dudgeon case was referred to the Court by the European Commission of Human Rights ('the Commission'). The case originated an application against the United Kingdom of Great Britain and Northern Ireland lodged with the Commission on May 22, 1976 under Article 25 of the Conventions for the Protection of Human Rights and Fundamental Freedoms ('the Convention') by a United Kingdom citizen, Mr Jeffrey Dudgeon.

2. The Commission's request was lodged with the registry of the Co. on July 18, 1980, within the period of three months laid down by Art. 32 para 1 and 47 (Art. 32 - 1, Art. 47). The request referred to Articles 44 and 48 and to the declaration made by the United Kingdom recognising the compulsory jurisdiction of the Court (Art. 46). The purpose of the Commission's request is to obtain a decision from the Court as to whether or not the facts of the case disclose a breach by the respondent State of its obligations under Art. 8 of the Convention, taken along in conjunction with Art. 14.

3. The Chamber of seven judges to be constituted included, as *ex-officio* members, Sir Vincent Evans, the elected judge of British nationality (Art. 43 of the Convention), and Mr G. Balladore Pallieri, the President of the Court (Rule 21 par. b of the Rules of Court). On September 30, 1980, the President drew by lot, in the presence of the Registrar, the names of the five other members of the Chamber, namely Mr G. Wiarda, Mr D. Evrigenis, Mr G. Lagergren, Mr L. Liesch and Mr J. Pinheiro Farinha (Art. 43 of the Convention and Rule 21 par. 4).

4. Mr Balladore Pallieri assumed the office of President of the Chamber (Rule 21 par. 5). He ascertained, through the Registrar, the views of the Agent of the Government of the United Kingdom ('the Government') and the Delegates of the Commission as regards the procedure to be followed. On October 24, 1980, he directed that the Agent of the Government should have, until December 24, 1980, to file a memorial and that the delegates should be entitled to file a memorial in reply within two months from the date of the transmission to them by the Registrar of the Government's memorial. On December 20, 1980, Mr Wiarda, the Vice-President of the Court, who had replaced Mr Balladore Pallieri as President of the Chamber following the latter's death (Rule 21 par. 5), agreed to extend the first of these time-limits until February 6, 1981.

5. On January 30, 1981, the Chamber decided under Rule 48 of the Rules of Court to relinquish jurisdiction forthwith in favour of the plenary Court.

6. The Government's memorial was received at the Registry on February 6, 1981, and that of the Commission on April 1, 1981.

Appended to the Commission's memorial were the applicant's observations on the Government's memorial.

7. After consulting through the Registrar, the Agent of the Government and the Delegates of the Commission, Mr Wiarda, who had in the meantime been elected President of the Court, directed on April 2, 1981, that the oral proceedings should open on April 23, 1981.

8. On April 3, 1981, the applicant invited the Court to hear expert evidence from Dr. Dannacker, Assistant Professor at the University of Frankfurt. In a letter received at the Registry on April 15, 1981, the Delegates of the Commission stated that they left it to the Court to decide whether such evidence was necessary.

9. A document was filed by the Government on April 14, 1981.

10. The oral hearings were held in public at the Human Rights Building, Strasbourg, on April 23, 1981. Immediately before their opening, the Court had held a preparatory meeting and decided not to hear expert evidence.

There appeared before the Court,

For the Government:

Mrs. A. Glover, Legal Advisor, Foreign and Commonwealth Office, Agent

Mr N. Bratza, Barrister-at-Law,
Mr B. Kerr, Barrister-at-Law, Counsel

Mr R. Tomlinson, Home Office,
Mr D. Chesterton, Northern Ireland Office,
Mr N. Bridges, Northern Ireland Office. Advisor

For the Commission:

Mr J. Fawcett,
Mr G. Tenekides, Delegate

Lord Gifford, Barrister-at-Law,
Mr T. Munyard, Barrister-at-Law,
Mr P. Crane, Solicitor, assisting the delegation under Rule 29 Par. second sentence, of the Rules of Court.

The Court heard addresses by the delegates and Lord Gifford for the Commission, and by Mr Kerr and Mr Bratza for the Government. Lord Gifford submitted various documents through the delegates of the Commission.

11. On May 11 and 12, 1981 respectively, the Registrar received from the Agent of the Government and from the Commission's delegates and those assisting them, written replies to certain questions put by the Court and/or their written observations on the documents filed before and during the hearings.

12. In September 1981, Mr Wiarda was prevented from taking part in consideration of the case; Mr Ryssdal, as Vice-President of the Court, thereafter presided over the Court.

AS TO THE FACTS

13. Mr Jeffrey Dudgeon, who is 35 years of age, is a shipping clerk, resident of Belfast, Northern Ireland.

Mr Dudgeon is a homosexual and his complaints are directed primarily against the existence in Northern Ireland of laws which have the effect of making certain homosexual acts between consenting adult males criminal offences.

A. THE RELEVANT LAW IN NORTHERN IRELAND

14. The relevant provisions currently in force in Northern Ireland contained in the Offences against the Person Act 1861 ('the 1861 Act'), the Criminal Law Amendment Act 1885 ('the 1855 Act') and the common law.

Under sections 61 and 62 of the 1861 Act, committing and attempting to commit buggery are made offences punishable with maximum sentences of life imprisonment and ten years' imprisonment, respectively. Buggery consists of sexual intercourse *per anum* by a man with a man or a woman, or *per anum* or *per vaginam* by a man or a woman with an animal.

By section 11 of the 1885 Act, it is an offence, punishable with a maximum of two years' imprisonment, for any male person, in public or in private, to commit an act of 'gross indecency' with another male. 'Gross indecency' is not statutorily defined but relates to any act involving sexual indecency between male persons, according to the evidence submitted to the Wolfenden Committee (see paragraph 17 below), it usually takes the form of mutual masturbation, inter-crural contact or oral-genital contact. At common law, an attempt to commit an offence is itself an offence and, accordingly, it is an offence to attempt to commit an act prescribed by Section of the 1885 Act. An attempt is in theory punishable in Northern Ireland by an unlimited sentence (but as to this, see paragraph 31 below).

Consent is no defence to any of these offences and no distinction regarding age is made in the text of the Acts.

An account of how the law is applied in practice is given below at paragraphs 29 to 31.

15. Acts of homosexuality between females are not, and have never been, criminal offences, although the offence of indecent assault may be committed by one woman on another under the age of 17.

As regards heterosexual relations, it is an offence, subject to certain exceptions, for a man to have sexual intercourse with a girl under the age of 17. Until 1950, the age of consent of a girl to sexual intercourse was 16 in both England and Wales and in Northern Ireland, but by legislations introduced in that year, the age of consent was increased to 17 in Northern Ireland. While in relation to the corresponding office in England and Wales it is a defence for a man under the age of 24 to show that he believed with reasonable cause the girl to be over 16 years of age, no such defence is available under Northern Ireland law.

B. THE LAW AND REFORM OF THE LAW IN THE REST OF THE UNITED KINGDOM

16. The 1861 and 1885 Acts were passed by the United Kingdom Parliament. When enacted, they applied to England and Wales, to all Ireland, then unpartitioned and an integral part of the United Kingdom, and also, in the case of the 1885 Act, to Scotland.

1. England and Wales

17. In England and Wales the current law on male homosexual acts are contained in the Sexual Offences Act 1956 ('the 1956 Act') as amended by the Sexual Offences Act 1967 ('the 1967 Act').

The 1956 Act, an Act consolidating the existing statute law, made it an offence for any person to commit buggery with another person or an animal (Section 12) and an offence for a man to commit an act of 'gross indecency' with another man (Section 13).

The 1967 Act, which was introduced into Parliament as a Private Member's Bill, was passed to give effect to the recommendations concerning homosexuality made in 1957 in the report of the Departmental Committee on Homosexual Offences and Prostitution established under the chairmanship of Sir John Wolfenden (the 'Wolfenden Committee' and 'Wolfenden Report'). The Wolfenden Committee regarded the function of the criminal law in this field as:

> 'to preserve public order and decency, to protect the citizen from what is offensive or injurious, and to provide sufficient safeguard against exploitation and corruption of others, particularly those who are specially vulnerable because they are young, weak in body or mind, inexperienced, or in a state of special physical, official, or economic dependence'.
>
> but not
>
> to intervene in the private lives of citizens, or to seek to enforce any particular pattern of behaviour, further than is necessary to carry out the purposes we have outlined.

The Wolfenden Committee concluded that homosexual behaviour between consenting adults in private was part of the 'realm of private morality and immorality which is, in brief and crude terms, not the law's business' and should no longer be criminal.

The 1967 Act qualified Sections 12 and 13 of the 1956 Act by providing that, subject to certain exceptions concerning mental patients, members of the armed forces and merchant seamen, buggery and acts of gross indecency in private between consenting males aged 21 years or over should not be criminal offences. It remains a crime to commit a homosexual act of the kind referred to in these sections, with a person aged less than 21 under any circumstances.

The age of majority for certain purposes, including capacity to marry without parental consent and to enter into contractual relations, was reduced from 21 to 18 by the Family Law Reform Act 1969. The voting age and the minimum age for jury service were likewise reduced to 18 by the Representation of the People Act 1969 and the Criminal Justice Act 1972, respectively.

In 1977, the House of Lords rejected a Bill aimed at reducing the age of consent for private homosexual act to 18. Subsequently, in report published in April 1981, a committee established by the Home Office, namely the Policy Advisory Committee on Sexual Offences, recommended that the minimum age for homosexual relations between males should be reduced to 18. A minority of five members favoured reduction to 16.

2. Scotland

18. When the applicant lodged his complaint in 1976, the relevant Act applicable was subsequently similar to that currently in force in Northern Ireland. Section 7 of the Sexual Offences (Scotland) Act 1976, a consolidating provision re-enacting Section 11 of the 1885 Act, provided for the offence of gross indecency, the offence of sodomy existed as common law. However, successive Lord Advocates stated in Parliament that their policy was not to prosecute in respect of acts which would not have been punishable if the 1967 Act had applied in Scotland. The Criminal Justice (Scotland) Act 1980 ('the 1980 Act') formally brought Scottish law into line with that of England and Wales. As in the case of the 1967 Act, the change in the law originated in amendments introduced in Parliament by a Private Member.

C. CONSTITUTIONAL POSITION OF NORTHERN IRELAND

19. Under an Act of the United Kingdom Parliament, the Government Ireland Act 1920, a separate Parliament for Northern Ireland was established with power to legislate on all matters developed by that Act, including criminal and social law. An executive known as the Government of Northern Ireland was also established with Ministers responsible for the different areas of the devolved powers. By convention, during the life of the Northern Ireland Parliament (1921-1972), the United Kingdom

Parliament rarely, if ever, legislated for Northern Ireland in respect of the devolved matters in particular social matters—falling within the former Parliament's legislative competence.

20. In March 1972, the Northern Ireland Parliament was prorogued and Northern Ireland was made subject to 'direct rule' from Westminster (see the judgement of January 18, 1978 in the case of Ireland v. the United Kingdom, Series A No. 25, pp. 10 and 20-21, par. 19 and 49). Since that date, except for a period of five months in 1974 when certain legislative and executive powers were devolved to a Northern Ireland Assembly and Executive, legislation for Northern Ireland in all fields has been the responsibility of the United Kingdom Parliament. There are 12 members of the United Kingdom House of Commons, out of a total of 635, who represent constituencies in Northern Ireland.

Under the provisions currently in force, power is conferred on Her Majesty to legislate for Northern Ireland by Order in Council. Save where there are reasons of urgency, no recommendation may be made to Majesty to make an Order in Council under these provisions unless a draft of the Order has been approved by each House of Parliament. It is the responsibility of the Government to prepare a draft Order and to lay it before Parliament for approval. A draft can only be approved or rejected in toto by Parliament, but not amended. The function of the Queen in Council in making an Order once it has been approved by Parliament is purely formal. In practice, much legislation for Northern Ireland is effected in this form rather than by means of an Act of Parliament.

D. PROPOSALS FOR REFORM IN NORTHERN IRELAND

21. No measures comparable to the 1967 Act were ever introduced in Northern Ireland Parliament either by the Government of Northern Ireland or by any Private Member.

22. In July 1976, following the failure of the Northern Ireland Constitutional Convention to work out a satisfactory form of devolved government for Northern Ireland, the then Secretary of State for Northern Ireland announced in Parliament that the United Kingdom Government would thenceforth by looking closely at the need for legislation in fields which it had previously

been thought appropriate to leave to a future devolved government, in particular with a view to bringing Northern Ireland law more closely into harmony with laws in other parts of the country. He cited homosexuality and divorce as possible areas for action. However, recognising the difficulties about such subjects in Northern Ireland, he indicated that he would welcome the views of the local people, including those of the Standing Advisory Commission on Human Rights, ('the Advisory Commission') and of Members of Parliament representing Northern Ireland constituencies.

23. The Advisory Commission, which is an independent statutory body was accordingly invited to consider the matter. As regards homosexual offences, the Advisory Commission received evidence from a number of persons and organisations, religious and secular. No representations were made by the Roman Catholic Church in Northern Ireland or by any of the 12 Northern Ireland Members of the United Kingdom House of Commons.

The Advisory Commission published its report in April 1977. The Advisory Commission concluded that most people did not regard it as satisfactory to retain the existing differences in the law with regard to homosexuality and that few only would be strongly opposed to changes bringing Northern Ireland law into conformity with that in England and Wales. On the other hand, it did not consider that there would be support for legislation which went further, in particular by lowering the age of consent. Its recommendations were that the law of Northern Ireland should be brought into line with the 1967 Act, but that future amendments to the 1967 Act should not automatically apply to Northern Ireland.

24. On July 27, 1978, the Government published a proposal for a draft, Homosexual Offences (Northern Ireland) Order 1978, the effect of which would have been to bring Northern Ireland law on the matter broadly into line with that of England and Wales. In particular, homosexual acts in private between two consenting male adults over the age of 21 would no longer have been punishable.

In a foreword to the proposal, the responsible Minister stated that the Government had always recognised that

> homosexuality is an issue about which some people in Northern Ireland hold strong conscientious or religious opinions.

He summarised the main arguments for and against reform as follows:

> In brief, there are two differing viewpoints. One, based on an interpretation of religious principles, holds that homosexual acts under any circumstances are immoral and that the criminal law should be used, by treating them as crimes, to enforce moral behaviour. The other view distinguishes between, on the one hand that area of private morality within which a homosexual individual can (as a matter of civil liberty) exercise his private right of conscience and, on the other hand, the area of public concern where the state ought and must use the law for the protection of society and in particular for the protection of children, those who are mentally retarded and others who are incapable of valid personal consent.
>
> I have during my discussions with religious and other groups heard both these viewpoints expressed with sincerity and I understand the convictions that underlie both points of view. There are in addition other considerations which must be taken into account. For example, it has been pointed out that the present law is difficult to enforce, that fear of exposure can make a homosexual particularly vulnerable to blackmail and that this fear of exposure can cause unhappiness not only for the homosexual himself but also for his family and friends.
>
> While recognising these differing viewpoints I believe we should not overlook the common ground. Most people will agree that the young must be given special protection, and most people will also agree that law should be capable of being enforced. Moreover those who are against reform have compassion and respect for individual rights just as much as those in favour of reform have concern for the welfare of society. For the individuals in society, as for Government, there is thus a difficult balance of judgment to be arrived at.

65. The applicant claimed to be a victim of discrimination in breach of Article 14 taken in conjunction with Article 8 (art. 14+8), in that he is subject under the criminal law complained of to greater interference with his private life than are male homosexuals in other parts of the United Kingdom and heterosexuals and female homosexuals in Northern Ireland itself. In particular, in his submission Article 14 requires that the age of consent should be the same for all forms of sexual relations.

66. When dealing with the issues under Article 14, the Commission and likewise, the Government distinguished between male homosexual acts involving those under and those over 21 years of age.

The Court has already held in relation to Article 8 that it falls in the first instance to the national authorities to fix the age under which young people should have the protection of the criminal law (see paragraph 62 above). The current law in Northern Ireland is silent in this respect as regards the male homosexual acts which it prohibits. It is only once this age has been fixed that an issue under Article 14 might arise; it is not for the Court to pronounce upon an issue which does not arise at the present moment.

67. Where a substantive Article of the Convention has been invoked both on its own and together with Article 14 and a separate breach has been found of the substantive Article, it is not generally necessary for the Court also to examine the case under Article 14, though the position is otherwise if a clear inequality of treatment in the enjoyment of the right in question is a fundamental aspect of the case (see the Airey judgment of October 9, 1979, Series A no. 32, p. 16, par. 30).

68. This latter condition is not fulfilled as regards the alleged discrimination resulting from the existence of different laws concerning male homosexual acts in various parts of the United Kingdom (see paragraphs 14, 17 and 18 above). Moreover, Mr Dudgeon himself conceded that, if the Court were to find a breach of Article 8 then this particular question would cease to have the same importance.

69. According to the applicant, the essential aspect of his complaint under Article 14 is that in Northern Ireland male

Public comment on the proposed amendment to the law was invited.

25. The numerous comments received by the Government in response to their invitation, during and after the formal period of consultation, revealed a substantial division of opinion. On a simple count of heads, there was a large majority of individuals and institutions against the proposal for a draft order.

Those opposed to reform included a number of senior Judges, District Councils, Orange Lodges and other organisations, generally of a religious character and in some cases engaged in youth activities. A petition to 'Save Ulster from Sodomy' organised by the Democratic Unionist Party led by Mr Ian Paisley, a Member of the United Kingdom House of Commons, collected nearly 70,000 signatures. The strongest opposition came from certain religious groups. In particular, the Roman Catholic bishops saw the proposal as an invitation to Northern Irish society to change radically its moral code in a manner liable to bring about more serious problems than anything attributable to the present law. The Roman Catholic bishops argued that such a change in the law would lead to a further decline in moral standards and to a climate of moral laxity which would endanger and put undesirable pressures on those most vulnerable, namely the young. Similarly, the Presbyterian Church in Ireland, whilst understanding the arguments for the change, made the point that the removal from the purview of the criminal law of private homosexual acts between consenting adult males might be taken by the public as an implicit license if not approval for such practices and as a change in public policy towards a further relaxation of moral standards.

The strongest support for change came from organisations representing homosexuals and social work agencies. They claimed that the existing law was unnecessary and that it created hardship and distress for a substantial minority of persons affected by it. It was urged that the sphere of morality should be kept distinct from that of the criminal law and that considerations of the personal freedom of the individual should in such matters be paramount. For its part, the Standing Committee of the General

Synod of the Church of Ireland accepted that homosexual acts in private between consenting adults aged 21 and over should be removed from the realm of criminal offence, but in amplification commented that this did not mean that the Church considered homosexuality to be an acceptable norm.

Press reports indicated that most of the political formations had expressed favourable views. However, none of the 12 Northern Ireland Members of Parliament publicly supported the proposed reform and several of them openly opposed it. An opinion poll conducted in Northern Ireland in January 1978, indicated that the people interviewed were evenly divided on the global question of the desirability of reforming the law on divorce and homosexuality so as to bring it into line with that of England and Wales.

26. On July 2, 1979, the then Secretary of State for Northern Ireland, in announcing to Parliament that the Government did not intend to pursue the proposed reform, stated:

Consultation showed that strong views are held in Northern Ireland, both for and against in the existing law. Although it is not possible to say with certainty what is the feeling of the majority of people in the province, it is clear that a substantial body of opinion there (embracing a wide range of religious as well as political opinion) is opposed to the proposed change...(T)he Government have (also) taken into account...the fact that legislation on an issue such as the one dealt with in the draft order has traditionally been a matter for the initiative of a Private Member rather than for the Government. At present, therefore, the Government propose to take no further action..., but we would be prepared to reconsider the matter if there were any developments in the future which were relevant.

27. In its annual report for 1979-1980, the Advisory Commission reiterated its view that law should be reformed. It believed that there was a danger that the volume of opposition might be exaggerated.

28. Since the Northern Ireland Parliament was prorogued in 1972 (see paragraph 20 above), there has been no initiative of any kind for legislation to amend the 1861 and 1885 Acts from

any of the mainstream political organisations or movements in Northern Ireland.

E. ENFORCEMENT OF THE LAW IN NORTHERN IRELAND

29. In accordance with the general law, anyone, including a private person, may bring a prosecution for a homosexual offence, subject to the Director of Public Prosecutions' power to assume the conduct of the proceedings and, if he thinks fit, discontinue them. The evidence as to prosecutions for homosexual offences between 1972 and 1981 reveals that none has been brought by a private person during that time.

30. During the period from January 1972 to October 1980 there were 62 prosecutions for homosexual offences in Northern Ireland. The majority of these cases involved minors, that is persons under 18, a few involved persons aged 18 to 21 or mental patients or prisoners. So far as the Government are aware from investigation of the records, no one was prosecuted in Northern Ireland during the period in question for an act which would clearly not have been an offence if committed in England or Wales. There is, however, no stated policy to prosecute in respect of such acts. As was explained to the Court by the Government, instructions operative within the office of the Director of Public Prosecutions reserve the decision on whether to prosecute in each individual case to the Director personally, in consultation with the Attorney General, the sole criterion being whether, on all the facts and circumstances of that case, a prosecution would be in public interest.

31. According to the Government, the maximum sentences prescribed in the 1861 and 1885 Acts are appropriate only for the most grave instances of the relevant offence and in practice, no court would ever contemplate imposing the maximum sentence for offences committed between consenting parties, whether in private or in public. Furthermore, although liable to an unlimited sentence, a minor convicted of an attempt to commit gross indecency would in practice never receive a sentence greater than that appropriate if the offence had been complete; in general, the sentence would be significantly less. In all cases of homosexual offences the actual penalty imposed will depend on the particular circumstances.

F. THE PERSONAL CIRCUMSTANCES OF THE APPLICANT

32. The applicant has, on his own evidence, been consciously homosexual from the age of 14. For some time he and others have been conducting a campaign aimed at bringing the law in Northern Ireland into line with that in force in England and Wales and, if possible, achieving a minimum age of consent lower than 21 years.

33. On January 21, 1976, the police went to Mr Dudgeon's address to execute a warrant under the Misuse of Drugs Act 1971. During the search of the house a quantity of cannabis was found which subsequently led to another person being charged with drug offences. Personal papers, including correspondence and diaries, belonging to the applicant in which were described homosexual activities were also found and seized. As a result, he was asked to go to a police station where for about four and a half hours he was questioned, about his sexual life. The police investigation file was sent to the Director of Prosecutions. It was considered with a view to instituting proceedings for the offence of gross indecency between males. The Director, in consultation with the Attorney General, decided that it would not be in public interest for proceedings to be brought. Mr Dudgeon was so informed in February 1977 and his papers, with annotations marked over them, were returned to him.

PROCEEDINGS BEFORE THE COMMISSION

34. In his application lodged with the Commission on May 22, 1976, Mr Dudgeon claimed that:

- the existence, in the criminal law in force in Northern Ireland, of various offences capable of relating to male homosexual conduct and the police investigation in January 1976 constituted an unjustified interference with his right to respect for his private life, in breach of Article 8 of the Convention;
- he had suffered discrimination, within the meaning of Article 14 of the Convention, on grounds of sex, sexuality and residence.

The applicant also claimed compensation.

35. By a decision of March 3, 1978, the Commission declared

admissible the applicant's complaints concerning the laws in force in Northern Ireland prohibiting homosexual acts between males (or attempts at as such acts), but his complaints concerning inadmissible by virtue of their being manifestly ill-founded the existence in Northern Ireland of certain common law offences.

In its report adopted on March 13, 1980, Article 31 of the Convention, the Commission expressed the opinion that:

- the legal prohibition of private consensual homosexual acts involving male persons under 21 years of age was not in breach of the applicant's rights either under Article 8 (eight votes to two) or under Article 14 read in conjunction with Article 8 (eight votes to one, with one abstention);
- the legal prohibition of such acts between male persons over 21 years of age breached the applicant's right to respect for his private life under Article 8 (nine votes to one);
- it was not necessary to examine the question whether the last-mentioned prohibition also violated Article 14 read in conjunction with Article 8 (nine votes to one).

The report contains one separate opinion.

FINAL SUBMISSIONS MADE TO THE COURT.

36. At the hearing on April 23, 1981, the Government maintained the submissions set out in their memorial, whereby they requested the Court:

(1) With regard to Article 8

To decide and declare that the present laws in Northern Ireland relating to homosexual acts do not give rise to a breach of Article 8 of the Convention, in that the laws are necessary in a democratic society for the protection of morals and for the protection of the rights of others for the purposes of paragraph 2 of Article 8.

(2) With regard to Article 14, in conjunction with Article 8.

(i) To decided and declare that the facts disclose no breach of Article 14, read in conjunction with Article 8 (Art. 14+8) of the Convention.

Alternatively, if and in so far as a breach of Article 8 of the Convention is found.

(ii) To decide and declare that it is unnecessary to examine the question whether the laws in Northern Ireland relating to homosexual acts give rise to a separate breach of Article 14, read in conjunction with Article 8 of the Convention.

AS TO THE LAW

I. THE ALLEGED BREACH OF ARTICLE 8

A. INTRODUCTION

37. The applicant complained that under the law in force in Northern Ireland he is liable to criminal prosecution on account of his homosexual conduct and that he has experienced fear, suffering and psychological distress directly caused by the very existence of the laws in question — including fear of harassment and blackmail. He further complained that, following the search of his house in January 1976, he was questioned by the police about certain homosexual activities and that personal papers belonging to him were seized during the search and not returned until more than a year later.

He alleged that, in breach of Article 8 of the Convention, he has thereby suffered, and continues to suffer, an unjustified interference with his right to respect for his private life.

38. Article 8 provides as follows:

1. Everyone has the right to respect for his private and family life, his home and his correspondence.
2. There shall be no interference by a public authority with the exercise of this right except such as is in accordance with the law and is necessary in a democratic society in the interests of national security, public safety or the economic well-being of the country, for the prevention of disorder or crime, for the protection of health or morals, or for the protection of the rights and freedoms of others.

39. Although it is not homosexuality itself which is prohibited but particular acts of gross indecency between males and buggery (see paragraph 14 above), there can be no doubt but

that male homosexual practices whose prohibition is the subject of the applicant's complaints come within the scope of the offences punishable under the impugned legislation; it is on that basis that the case has been argued by the Government, the applicant and the Commission. Furthermore, the offences are committed whether the act takes place in public or in private, whatever the age or relationship of the participants involved, and whether or not the participants are consenting. It is evident from Mr Dudgeon's submissions, however, that his complaint was in essence directed against the fact that homosexual acts which he might commit in private with other males capable of valid consent are criminal offences under the law of Northern Ireland.

B. THE EXISTENCE OF AN INTERFERENCE WITH AN ARTICLE 8. RIGHT

40. The Commission saw no reason to doubt the general truth of the applicant's allegations concerning the fear and distress that he had suffered in consequence of the existence of the laws in question. Commission unanimously concluded that 'the legislation complained of interference with the applicant's right to respect for his private life guaranteed by Article 8 par. 1, in so far as it prohibits homosexual acts committed in private between consenting males' (see paragraphs 94 and 97 of the Commission's report).

The Government, without conceding the point, did not dispute that Mr Dudgeon is directly affected by the laws and entitled to claim to be a 'victim' thereof under Article 25 of the Convention. Nor did the Government contest the Commission's above-quoted conclusion.

41. The Court sees no reason to differ from the views of the Commission: the maintenance in force of the impugned legislation constitutes a continuing interference with the applicant's right to respect for his private life (which includes his sexual life) within the meaning of Article 8 par. 1. In the personal circumstances of the applicant, the very existence of this legislation continuously and directly affects his private life (see, *mutatis mutandis*, the Marckx judgement of June 13, 1979, Series A no. 31, par. 27): either he respects the law and refrains from

engaging — even in private with consenting male partners — in prohibited sexual acts to which he is disposed by reason of his homosexual tendencies, or commits such acts and thereby becomes liable to criminal prosecution.

It cannot be said that the law in question is a dead letter in this sphere. It was, and still is, applied so as to prosecute persons with regard to private consensual homosexual acts involving males under 21 years of age. Although no proceedings seem to have been brought in recent years with regard to such acts involving only males over 21 years of age, apart from mental patients, there is no stated policy on the part of the authorities not to enforce the law in this respect (see paragraph 30 above). Furthermore, apart from prosecution by the Director of Public Prosecution, there always remains the possibility of a private prosecution (see paragraph 29 above).

Moreover, the police investigation in January 1976 was, in relation to the legislation in question, a specific measure of implementation — albeit short of actual prosecution — which directly affected the applicant in the enjoyment of his right to respect for his private life (see paragraph 33 above). As such, it showed that the threat hanging over him was real.

C. THE EXISTENCE OF A JUSTIFICATION FOR THE INTERFERENCE FOUND BY THE COURT

42. In the Government's submission, the law in Northern Ireland relating to homosexual acts does not give rise to a breach of Article 8 in that it is justified by the terms of paragraph 2 of the Article. This contention was disputed by both the applicant and the Commission.

43. An interference with the exercise of an Article 8 right will not be compatible with paragraph 2 unless it is 'in accordance with the law', has an aim or aims that is or are legitimate under that paragraph and is 'necessary in a democratic society' for the aforesaid aim or aims (see, mutatis, mutandis, the Young, James and Webster judgment of August 13, 1981, Series A no. 4 p. 24, par. 59).

44. It has not been contested that the first of these three conditions was met. As the Commission pointed out in paragraph

99 of its report, the interference is plainly 'in accordance with the law' since it results from the existence of certain provisions in the 1861 and 1885 Acts and the common law (see paragraph 14 above).

45. It next falls to be determined whether the interference is aimed at 'the protection of morals' or 'the protection of the rights and freedoms of others', the two purposes relied on by the Government.

46. The 1861 and 1885 Acts were passed in order to enforce the then prevailing conception of sexual morality. Originally they applied to England and Wales, to all Ireland, then unpartitioned, and also, in case of the 1885 Act, to Scotland (see paragraph 16 above). In recent years the scope of the legislation has been restricted to England and Wales (with the 1967 Act) and subsequently to Scotland (with the 1980 Act), with certain exceptions it is no longer a criminal offence for two consenting males over 21 years of age to commit homosexual acts in private (see paragraphs 17 and 18 above). In Northern Ireland, in contrast, the law has remained unchanged. The decision announced in July 1979 to take no further action in relation to the proposal to amend the existing law was, the Court accepts, prompted by what the United Kingdom Government judged to be the strength of feeling in Northern Ireland against the proposed change, and in particular the strength of the view that it would be seriously damaging to the moral fabric of Northern Irish society (see paragraphs 25 and 26 above). This being so, the general aim pursued by the legislation remains the protection of morals in the sense of moral standards obtaining in Northern Ireland.

47. Both the Commission and the Government took the view that, in as far as the legislation seeks to safeguard young persons from undesirable and harmful pressures and attentions, it is also aimed at 'the protection of the rights and freedoms of others'. The Court recognises that one of the purposes of the legislation is to afford safeguards for vulnerable members of society, such as the young, against the consequences of homosexual practices. However, it is some what artificial in this context to draw a rigid distinction between 'protection of the rights and freedoms of others' and 'protection of morals'. The

latter may imply safeguarding the moral ethos or moral standards of a society as a whole (see paragraph 108 of the Commission's report), but may also, as the Government pointed out, cover protection of the moral interests and welfare of a particular section of society, for example school children (see the Handyside judgment of December 7, 1976, Series A no. 24, p. 25, par. 52 in fine — in relation to Article 10 par. 2 of the Convention). Thus, protection of the rights and freedoms of others', when meaning the safeguarding of the moral interests and welfare of certain individuals or classes of individuals who are in need of special protection for reasons such as lack of maturity, mental disability or state of dependence, amounting to one aspect of 'protection of morals' (see, *mutatis mutandis, the Sunday Times* judgment of April 5, 1979, Series A no. 30, p. 34, par. 56). The Court will therefore take into account the two aims on this basis.

48. As the Commission rightly observed in its report (at paragraph 101), the cardinal issue arising under Article 8 in this case is to what extent, if at all, the maintenance in force by the legislation is 'necessary in a democratic society' for these aims.

49. There can be no denial that some degree of regulation of male homosexual conduct, as indeed of other forms of sexual conduct, by means of the criminal law can be justified as 'necessary in a democratic society'. The overall function served by the criminal law in this field is, in the words of the Wolfenden report (see paragraph 17 above), 'to preserve public order and decency [and] to protect the citizen from what is offensive or injurious'. Furthermore, this necessity for some degree of control may even extend to consensual acts committed in private, notably where there is call — to quote the Wolfenden report once more— 'to provide sufficient safeguards against exploitation and corruption of others particularly those who are specially vulnerable because they are young, weak in body or mind, inexperienced, or in a state of special physical, official or economic dependence.' In practice, there is legislation on the matter in all the member States of the Council of Europe, but what distinguishes the law in Northern Ireland from that existing in the great majority of the member States is that it prohibits generally gross indecency between males and buggery whatever

the circumstances. It being accepted that some form of legislation is 'necessary' to protect particular sections of society as well as the moral ethos of society as a whole, the question in the present case is whether the contested provisions of the law of Northern Ireland and their enforcement remain within the bounds of what, in a democratic society, may be regarded as necessary in order to accomplish those aims.

50. A number of principles relevant to the assessment of the 'necessity', 'in a democratic society', of a measure taken in furtherance of an aim that is legitimate under the Convention have been stated by the Court in previous judgments.

51. Firstly, 'necessary' in this context does not have the flexibility of such expressions as 'useful', 'reasonable', or 'desirable', but implies the existence of a 'pressing social need' for the interference in question (see the above-mentioned Handyside judgment, p. 22, par. 48).

52. In the second place, it is for the national authorities to make the initial assessment of the pressing social need in each case; accordingly, a margin of appreciation is left to them (Handyside judgment). However, their decision remains subject to review by the Court. (ibid., p. 23, par. 49).

As was illustrated by the *Sunday Times* judgment, the scope of the margin of appreciation is not identical in respect of each of the aims justifying restrictions on a right (p. 36, par. 59). The Government inferred from the Handyside judgment that the margin of appreciation will be more extensive where the protection of morals is in issue. It is an indisputable fact, as the Court stated in the Handyside judgment, that 'the view taken... of the requirements of morals vary from time to time and from place to place, especially in our era,' and that 'by reason of their direct and continuous contact with the vital forces of their countries, State authorities are in principle, in a better position than the international judge to give an opinion on the exact content of those requirements' (p. 22, par. 48).

However, not only the nature of the aim of the restriction but also nature of the activities involved will affect the scope of the margin of appreciation. The present case concerns a most intimate aspect of private life. Accordingly, there must exist particularly serious reasons before interferences on the part of the public authorities can be legitimate for the purposes of paragraph 2 of Article 8.

53. Finally, in Article 8 as in several other Articles of the Convention, the notion of 'necessity' is linked to that of a 'democratic society'. According to the Court's case-law, a restriction on a Convention right cannot be regarded as 'necessary in a democratic society' — two hallmarks of which are tolerance and broad-mindedness unless, amongst other things, it is proportionate to the legitimate aim pursued (see the above-mentioned Handyside judgment, p. 23, par. 49, and the above-mentioned Young, James and Webster judgment, p. 25, par. 63).

54. The Court's task is to determine on the basis of the aforestated principles whether the reasons purporting to justify the 'interference' in question are relevant and sufficient under Article 8 par. 2 (see the above-mentioned Handyside judgment, pp. 23-24, par. 50). The Court is not concerned with making any value-judgment as to the morality of homosexual relations between adult males.

55. It is convenient to begin by examining the reasons set out by Government in their arguments contesting the Commission's conclusion that the penal prohibition of private consensual homosexual acts involving male persons over 21 years of age is not justified under Article 8 par. 2 (see paragraph 35 above).

56. In the first place, the Government drew attention to what they described as profound differences of attitude and public opinion between Northern Ireland and Great Britain in relation to questions of morality. Northern Irish society was said to be more conservative and to place greater emphasis on religious factors, as was illustrated by more restrictive laws even in the field of heterosexual conduct (see paragraph 15 above).

Although the applicant qualified this account of the facts as grossly exaggerated, the Court acknowledges that such differences do exist to a certain extent and are a relevant factor. As the Government and the Commission both emphasised, in assessing the requirements of the protection of morals in Northern

Ireland, the contested measures must be seen in the context of Northern Irish society.

The fact that similar measures are not considered necessary in other parts of the United Kingdom or in other member States of the Council of Europe does not mean that they cannot be necessary in Northern Ireland (see, *mutatis mutandis*, the above-mentioned *Sunday Times* judgment, pp. 37-38, par. 61, cf. also the above-mentioned Handyside judgment, pp. 26-28, par. 54 and 57). Where there are disparate cultural communities residing within the same State, it may well be that different requirements, both moral and social, will face the governing authorities.

57. As the Government correctly submitted, it follows that the moral climate in Northern Ireland in sexual matters, in particular as evidenced by the opposition to the proposed legislative change, is one of the matters which the national authorities may legitimately take into account in exercising their discretion. There is, the Court accepts, a strong body of opposition stemming from a genuine and sincere conviction shared by a large number of responsible members of the Northern Irish community that a change in the law would be seriously damaging to the moral fabric of society (see paragraph 25 above). This opposition reflects — as do in another way the recommendations made in 1977 by the Advisory Commission (see paragraph 23 above) a view both of the requirements of morals in Northern Ireland and of the measures thought within the community to be necessary to preserve prevailing moral standards.

Whether this point of view be right or wrong, and although it may be of line with current attitudes in other communities, its existence among the important sector of Northern Irish society is certainly relevant for the purposes of Article 8 par. 2.

58. The Government argued that this conclusion is further strengthened by the special constitutional circumstances of Northern Ireland (described above at paragraphs 19 and 20). In the period between 1921 (when the Northern Ireland Parliament first met) and 1972 (when it last sat), legislation in the social field was regarded as a devolved matter within the exclusive domain of that Parliament. As a result of the introduction of 'direct rule' from Westminster, the United Kingdom Government, it was said,

had a special responsibility to take full account of the wishes of the people of Northern Ireland before legislating on such matters.

In the present circumstances of direct rule, the need for caution and for sensitivity to public opinion in Northern Ireland is evident. However, the Court does not consider it conclusive in assessing the 'necessity', for the purposes of the Convention, of maintaining the impugned legislation that the decision was taken, not by the former Northern Ireland Government and Parliament, but by the United Kingdom authorities during what they hope to be an interim period of direct rule.

59. Without any doubt, faced with these various considerations, the United Kingdom Government acted carefully and in good faith; what is more, they made every effort to arrive at a balanced judgment between the differing viewpoints before reaching the conclusion that such a substantial body of opinion in Northern Ireland was opposed to a change in the law that no further action should be taken (see, for example, paragraphs 24 and 26 above). Nevertheless, this cannot of itself be decisive as to the necessity for the interference with the applicant's private life resulting from the measures being challenged (see the above-mentioned *Sunday Times* judgment, p. 36, par. 59). Notwithstanding the margin of appreciation left to the national authorities, it is for the Court to make the final evaluation as to whether the reasons it has found to be relevant were sufficient in the circumstances, in particular whether the interference complained of was proportionate to the social need claimed for it (see paragraph 53 above).

60. The Government's right affected by the impugned legislation protects an essentially private manifestation of the human personality (see paragraph 52, third sub-paragraph, above).

As compared with the era when that legislation was enacted, there is a better understanding, and in consequence an increased tolerance, of homosexual behaviour to the extent that in the great majority of the member states of the Council of Europe it is no longer considered necessary or appropriate to treat homosexual practices of the kind now in question as in themselves a matter to which the sanctions of the criminal law should be applied; the

Court cannot overlook the marked changes which have occurred in this regard in the domestic law of the member states (see, *mutatis mutandis*, the above-mentioned Marckx judgment, p. 19, par. 41, and the Tyrer judgment of April 25, 1978, Series A no. 26, pp. 15-16, par. 31). In Northern Ireland itself, the authorities have refrained in recent years from enforcing the law in respect of private homosexual acts between consenting males over the age of 21 years capable of valid consent (see paragraph 30 above). No evidence has been adduced to show that this has been injurious to moral standards in Northern Ireland or that there has been any public demand for stricter enforcement of the law.

It cannot be maintained in these circumstances that there is a 'pressing social need' to make such acts criminal offences, there being no sufficient justification provided by the risk of harm to vulnerable sections of society requiring protection or by the effects on the public. On the issue of proportionality, the Court considers that such justifications as there are for retaining the law in force unamended are outweighed by the detrimental effects which the very existence of the legislative provisions in question have on the life of a person of homosexual orientation like the applicant. Although members of the public who regard homosexuality as immoral may be shocked, offended or disturbed by the commission by others of private homosexual acts, this cannot on its own warrant the application of penal sanctions when it is consenting adults alone who are involved.

61. Accordingly, the reasons given by the Government, although relevant, are not sufficient to justify the maintenance in force of the impugned legislation in so far as it has the general effect of criminalising private homosexual relations between adult males capable of valid consent. In particular, the moral attitudes towards male homosexuality in Northern Ireland and the concern that any relaxation in the law would tend to erode existing moral standards cannot, without more, warrant interfering with the applicant's private life to such an extent. 'Decriminalisation' does not imply approval, and a fear that some sectors of the population might draw misguided conclusions in this respect from reform of the legislation does not afford a good ground for maintaining it in force with all unjustifiable features.

To sum up, the restriction imposed on Mr Dudgeon under Northern Ireland law, by reason of its breadth and absolute character, is, quite apart from the severity of the possible penalties provided for, disproportionate to the aims sought to be achieved.

62. In the opinion of the Commission, the interference complained by the applicant can, in so far as he is prevented from having sexual relations with young males under 21 years of age, be justified as necessary for the protection of the rights of others (see especially paragraphs 105 and 116 of the report). This conclusion was accepted and adopted by the Government, but disputed by the applicant who submitted that the age of consent for male homosexual relations should be the same as that for heterosexual and female homosexual relation that is, 17 years under current Northern Ireland law (see paragraph above).

The Court has already acknowledged the legitimate necessity in a democratic society for some degree of control over homosexual conduct notably in order to provide safeguards against the exploitation and corruption of those who are specially vulnerable by reason, for example, of their youth (see paragraph 49 above). However, it falls in the first instance to the national authorities to decide on the appropriate safeguards of this kind required for the defence of morals in their society and, in particular, to fix the age under which young people should have the protection of the criminal law (see paragraph 52 above).

D. CONCLUSION

63. Mr Dudgeon has suffered and continues to suffer an unjustified interference with his right to respect for his private life, a breach of Article 8.

II. THE ALLEGED BREACH OF ARTICLE 14 TAKEN IN CONJUNCTION

64. Article 14 reads as follows:

> The enjoyment of the rights and freedoms set forth in this Convention shall be secured without discrimination on any ground such as sex, race, colour, language, religion, political or other opinion, national or social origin, association, with a national minority, property, birth or other status.

homosexual acts, in contrast to heterosexual and female homosexual acts, are the object of criminal sanctions even when committed in private between consenting adults.

The central issue in the present case does indeed reside in the existence in Northern Ireland of legislation which makes certain homosexual acts punishable under the criminal law in all circumstances. Nevertheless, this aspect of the applicant's complaint under Article 14 amounts in effect to the same complaint, albeit seen from a different angle, that the Court already considered in relation to Article 8, there is no cause to rule on the merits of a particular issue which is part of and absorbed by a wider issue (see, *mutatis mutandis*, the Deweer judgment of February 27, 1980, Series A no. 35, pp. 30-31, par. 56 in fine). Once it has been held that the restriction on the applicant's right of respect for his private sexual life give rise to a breach of Article 8 by reason of its breadth and absolute character (see paragraph 61 in fine above), there is no useful legal purpose to be served in determining whether he has in addition suffered discrimination as compared with other persons who are subject to lesser limitations on the same right. This being so, it cannot be said that a clear inequality of treatment remains a fundamental aspect of the case.

70. The Court accordingly does not deem it necessary to examine the case under Article 14 as well.

III. The application of Article 50 (Art. 50)

71. Counsel for the applicant stated that, should the Court find the Convention to have been violated, his client would seek just satisfaction under Article 50 in respect of three matters. Firstly, the distress, suffering and anxiety resulting from the police investigation in January 1976; secondly, the general fear and distress suffered by Mr Dudgeon since he was 17 years of age; and finally, legal and other expenses. Counsel put forward figures of 5,000 pounds under the first head, 10,000 pounds under the second and 5,000 pounds under the third.

The Government, for their part, asked the Court to reserve the question.

72. Consequently, although it was raised under Rule 47 bis of the Rules of Court, this question is not ready for decision and must be reserved; in the circumstances of the case, the Court considers that the matter should be referred back to the Chamber in accordance with Rule 50 par. 4 of the Rules of Court.

FOR THE REASONS, THE COURT

1. Holds by fifteen votes to four that there is a breach of Article 8 of the Convention;
2. Holds by fourteen votes to five that it is not necessary also to examine the case under Article 14 taken in conjunction with Article 8;
3. Holds unanimously that the question of the application of Article 50 is not ready for decision:
   (a) accordingly reserves the whole of the said question;
   (b) refers the said question back to the Chamber under Rule 50 par. 4 of the Rules of Court.

Done in English and in French, the English text being authentic, at Human Rights Building, Strasbourg, this twenty-second day of October, one thousand nine hundred and eighty-one.

For the President
Signed: John Cremona
Judge
Signed: Marc-André Eissen
Registrar

The following separate opinions are annexed to the present judgment in accordance with Article 51 par. 2 of the Convention and Rule 50 par. 2 of the Rules of Court:

— dissenting opinion of Mr Zekia;
— dissenting opinion of Mr Evrigenis and Mr Garcia de Enterria;
— dissenting opinion of Mr Matscher;
— dissenting opinion of Mr Pinheiro Farinha;
— partially dissenting opinion of Mr Walsh.

Initialled: J. C.
Initialled: M.A.E.

DISSENTING OPINION OF JUDGE ZEKIA

I am dealing only with the crucial point which led the Court to find a breach of Article 8 § 1 of the Convention by the responding Government.

The Acts of 1861 and 1885 still in force in Northern Ireland prohibit gross indecency between males and buggery. These enactments in their unamended form are found to interfere with the right to respect for the private life of the applicant, admittedly a homosexual.

The decisive central issue in this case is therefore whether the provisions of the aforesaid laws criminalising homosexual relations were necessary in a democratic society for the protection of morals and for the protection of the rights and freedoms of others, such a necessity being a prerequisite for the validity of the enactment under Article 8 § 2 of the Convention.

After taking all relevant facts and submissions made in this case into consideration, I have arrived at a conclusion opposite to the one of the majority. I proceed to give my reasons as briefly as possible for finding no violation on the part of the respondent Government in this case.

1. Christian and Moslem religions are all united in the condemnation of homosexual relations and of sodomy. Moral conceptions to a great degree are rooted in religious beliefs.

2. All civilised countries until recent years penalised sodomy and buggery and akin unnatural practices.

In Cyprus, criminal provisions similar to those embodied in the Acts of 1861 and 1885 in the North of Ireland are in force. Section 171 of the Cyprus Criminal Code, Cap. 154, which was enacted in 1929, reads:

'Any person who

(a) has carnal knowledge of any person against the order of nature, or

(b) permits a male person to have carnal knowledge of him against the order of nature

is guilty of felony and is liable to imprisonment for five years.

Under section 173, anyone who attempts to commit such an offence is liable to 3 years' imprisonment.

While on the one hand I may be thought biased for being a Cypriot Judge, on the other hand I may be considered to be in a better position in forecasting the public outcry and the turmoil which would ensue if such laws are repealed or amended in favour of homosexuals either in Cyprus or in Northern Ireland. Both countries are religious-minded and adhere to moral standards which are centuries' old.

3. While considering the respect due to the private life of a homosexual under Article 8 § 1 we must not forget and must bear in mind that respect is also due to the people holding the opposite view, especially in a country populated by a great majority of such people who are completely against unnatural, immoral practices. Surely the majority in a democratic society are also entitled under Articles 8, 9 and 10 of the Convention and Article 2 of Protocol No. 1 (P 1-2) to respect for their religious and moral beliefs and entitled to teach and bring up their children consistently with their own religious and philosophical convictions.

A democratic society is governed by the rule of the majority

It seems to me somewhat odd and perplexing, in considering the necessity of respect for one's private life, to underestimate the necessity of keeping a law in force for the protection of morals held in high esteem by the majority of people.

A change of the law so as to legalise homosexual activities in private by adults is very likely to cause many disturbances in the country in question. The respondent Government were justified in finding it necessary to keep the relevant Acts on the statute book for the protection of morals as well as for the preservation of public peace.

4. If a homosexual claims to be a sufferer because of physiological, psychological or other reasons and the law ignores such circumstances his case might then be one of exculpation or mitigation if his tendencies are curable or incurable. Neither of these arguments has been put forward or contested. Had the applicant done so, then his domestic remedies ought to have been exhausted. In fact he has not been prosecuted for any offence.

From the proceedings in this case it is evident that what the applicant is claiming by virtue of Article 8 § 1 and 2 of the European

Convention is to be free to indulge privately in homosexual relations.

Much has been said about the scarcity of cases coming to court under the prohibitive provisions of the Acts we are discussing. It was contended that this fact indicates the indifference of the people in Northern Ireland to the non-prosecution of homosexual offences committed. The same fact, however, might indicate the rarity of homosexual offences having been perpetrated and also the unnecessariness and the inexpediency of changing the law.

5. In ascertaining the nature and scope of morals and the degree of the necessity commensurate to the protection of such morals in relation to a national law, adverted to in Articles 8, 9 and 10 of the European Convention on Human Rights, the jurisprudence of this Court has already provided us with guidelines:

"A" The conception of morals changes from time to time and from place to place. There is no uniform European conception of morals. State authorities of each country are in a better position than an international judge to give an opinion as to the prevailing standards of morals in their country. (Handyside judgment of December 7, 1976, Series A no. 24, p. 22 § 48)

It cannot be disputed that the moral climate obtaining in Northern Ireland is against the alteration of the law under consideration, the effect of which alteration, if made, would be in some way or other to license immorality.

"B" State authorities likewise are in a better position to assess the extent to which the national legislation should necessarily go in restricting, for the protection of morals and of the rights of others, rights secured under the relevant Articles of the Convention.

The legislative assembly competent to alter the laws under review refrained to do so, believing it to be necessary to maintain them for the protection of morals prevailing in the region and for keeping the peace. The contracting states are entitled to a margin of appreciation, although undoubtedly not an unlimited one.

Taking account of all relevant facts and points of law and

the underlying principles for an overall assessment of the situation under consideration, I fail to find that the keeping in force in Northern Ireland of Acts — which date from the last century — prohibiting gross indecency and buggery between male adults has become unnecessary for the protection of morals and of the rights of others in that country. I have come to the conclusion therefore that the respondent Government did not violate the Convention.

DISSENTING OPINION OF JUDGES EVRIGENIS AND GARCIA DE ENTERRIA

(Translation)

Being of the opinion that the case should also have been examined under Article 14 read in conjunction with Article 8 but without prejudging our position on the merits of the matter, we have felt compelled to vote against point no. 2 in the operative provisions of the judgment for the following reasons.

At least the difference of treatment in Northern Ireland between male homosexuals and female homosexuals and between male homosexual and heterosexuals (see paragraphs 65 and 69 of the judgment) — a difference in treatment relied on in argument by the applicant — ought to have been examined under Article 14 read in conjunction with Article 8. Even accepting the restrictive formula enunciated by the Court in the Airey judgment and applied in the judgment in the present case (at paragraph 67: 'a clear inequality of treatment being a fundamental aspect of the case' would be difficult to assert that these conditions were not plainly satisfied in the circumstances. In any event, to interpret Article 14 in the restrictive manner heralded in the Airey judgment deprives this fundamental provision in great part of its substance function in the system of substantive rules established under the Convention.

DISSENTING OPINION OF JUDGE MATSCHER

(Translation)

I. As concerns the alleged interference with an Article 8 right

Although I agree with the general tenor of the Court's reasoning, I take a somewhat different view of the facts of the case. As a result, I am unable to concur with the conclusions of the judgment on the issue of a violation of Article 8 of the Convention. I will therefore endeavour to set out my views below.

Article 8 does not at all require that the State should consider homosexuality in whatever form it may be manifested — as an alternative that is equivalent to heterosexuality and that, in consequence, its laws should treat each of them on the same footing. Indeed, the judgment quite rightly adverts to this point on several occasions.

On the other hand, it does not follow from the above that the criminal prosecution of homosexual acts committed in private between consenting adults (leaving aside certain special situations as, for example, where there has been abuse of a state of dependence or where the acts occur in certain contexts of communal living such as a boarding school, barracks, etc.) is 'necessary', within the meaning of Article 8 § 2 for the protection of those values which a given society legitimately (likewise for the purposes of the Convention) wishes to preserve. I therefore agree with the general tenor of the reasoning in the judgment as regards the interpretation to be given to Article 8 and in particular to paragraph 2 of that Article in the present case.

In this connection, however, there are two arguments to which I cannot subscribe.

At paragraph 51, it is said that the adjective 'necessary' implies the existence of a 'pressing social need' for the interference in question (reference to the Handyside judgment of December 7, 1976 Series A no. 24 § 48). To my mind, however, once it has been granted that an aim is legitimate for the purposes of Article 8 § 2 any measure directed towards the accomplishment of that aim is necessary if failure to take the measure would create a risk that aim would not be achieved. It is only in this context that one can examine the necessity for a certain measure and, adding a further factor, the proportionality between the value attaching to aim and the seriousness of the measure (see paragraphs 54 and 60 in fine). Since the adjective 'necessary' thus refers solely to the measures (that is, the means), it does not permit an assessment whether the aim itself is legitimate, something that the judgement appears to do when it links 'necessary' with 'pressing social need'.

Furthermore, according to paragraph 60, second sub-paragraph, no evidence has been adduced to show that the attitude of tolerance adopted in practice by the Northern Ireland authorities has been injurious to moral standards in the region. I cannot but regard this as a purely speculative argument, devoid of any foundation and which thus has no probative value whatsoever.

My disagreement relates in the first place to the evaluation made of the legal provisions and the measures of implementation of which the applicant complains to have been a victim in *concreto* and to be still a potential victim by reason of the existence of the impugned legislation.

(a) The Government asserted that for a long time (to be precise, between 1972 and 1980) there have been no criminal prosecutions in circumstances corresponding to those of the present case. No one contradicted this assertion which, moreover, would more than appear to be a correct statement of the reality. It is true that at common law a prosecution could also be brought by a private individual, subject to the Director of Public Prosecutions' power to discontinue the proceedings. However, here again there have been no examples of prosecutions of this kind during the period in question (paragraphs 29-30).

I conclude from this that in practice there are no prosecutions for homosexual acts committed in private between consenting adults. The absence of any form of persecution seems to be well established by the existence of a number of associations (the Commission lists at least five in paragraph 30 of its report) — the applicant being the Secretary of one of them — which pursue their activities hardly in secret but more or less without any constraint and are, amongst other things, engaged in conducting a campaign for the legalisation of homosexuality and some of whose members, if not the majority, openly profess — it may be supposed — homosexual tendencies.

In these circumstances, the existence of 'fear, suffering and psychological distress' experienced by the applicant as a direct result of the laws in force — something which the Commission and the Court saw no reason of doubt (paragraphs 40-41) — seems to me, on the contrary, to be extremely unlikely.

To sum up, I believe that it is not the letter of the law that has to be taken into account, but the actual situation obtaining in Northern Ireland, that is to say, the attitude in fact adopted for at least ten years by the competent authorities in respect of male homosexuality.

The situation is therefore fundamentally different from that in the Marckx case (paragraph 27 of the judgment of June 13, 1979, Series A no. 31) to which the present judgment refers (in paragraph 41). In the former case, the provisions of Belgian civil law complained of being applied directly to the applicant who suffered their consequences in her family life; in the instant case, the legislation complained of is formally in force but as a matter of fact it is not applied as regards those of its aspects which are being attacked. This being so, the applicant and those like him can organise their private life as they choose without any interference on the part of the authorities.

Of course, the applicant and the organisations behind him are seeking more: they are seeking the express and formal repeal of the laws in force, that is to say a 'charter' declaring homosexuality to be an alternative equivalent to heterosexuality, with all the consequences that would entail (for example, as regards sex education). However, this is in no way required by Article 8 of the Convention.

(b) The police action on January 21, 1976 (paragraphs 30-31) again on the applicant can also be seen in a different light: in the particular circumstances, the police were executing a warrant under the Misuse of Drugs Act 1971. During the search, the police found papers providing evidence of his homosexual tendencies. The reason why the police pursued their enquiries was probably also to investigate whether the applicant did not have homosexual relations with minors as well. Indeed, it is well-known that this is a widespread tendency in homosexual circles and the fact that the applicant himself was engaged in a campaign for the lowering of the legal age of consent points in the same direction; furthermore, the enquiries in question took place in the context of a more extensive operation on the part of the police, the purpose of which was to trace a minor who was missing from home and believed to be associating with homosexuals (see on this point the reply of the Government to question 8, document Cour (81) 32). Furthermore, the file on the case was closed by the competent judicial authorities. This overall evaluation of the facts leads me to the view that the applicant cannot claim to be the victim of an interference with his private life. For this reason I conclude that there has not been a violation of Article 8 of the Convention in the present case.

II. As concerns the alleged breach of Article 14 read in conjunction with Article 8

The applicant alleged a breach of Article 14 read in conjunction with Article 8 on three (or even four) counts: (a) the existence of different laws in the different parts of the United Kingdom; (b) distinctions drawn in respect of the age of consent; (c) and (d) differences of treatment under the criminal law between male homosexuality and female homosexuality and between homosexuality and heterosexuality.

As far as the age of consent is concerned ((b)), the Court rightly notes (at paragraph 66, second sub-paragraph) that this is a matter to be fixed in the first instance by the national authorities. The reasoning of the majority of the Court runs as follows: male homosexuality is made punishable under the criminal law in Northern Ireland without any distinction as to the age of the persons involved. Consequently, it is only once this age has been fixed that an issue under Article 14 might arise. This reasoning is coherent and there is nothing to add.

To my mind, the competent authorities do in fact draw a distinction according to age and exhibit tolerance only in relation to homosexuality between consenting adults. I find that, for reasons whose obviousness renders any explanation superfluous, this differentiation is perfectly legitimate for the purposes of Article 14 and thus gives rise to no discrimination.

As regards the other complaints ((a), (c) and (d)), the majority of the Court state that when a separate breach of a substantive Article of the Convention has been found, there is generally no need for the Court also to examine the case under Article 14; the position is otherwise only if a clear inequality of treatment in the enjoyment of the right at issue is a fundamental aspect of the case (reference to the Airey judgment of October 9, 1979 Series A no. 32, paragraph 30). This latter condition is said not to be fulfilled in the circumstances. Furthermore, the judgment continues, there is no call to rule on the merits of a particular issue which is part of and absorbed by a wider issue (reference to the Deweer judgment of February 27, 1980, Series A no. 35, paragraph 56 in fine), this being the position in the present case. In these conditions, there appeared to the majority to be no useful legal purpose to be served in determining whether the applicant has in addition suffered discrimination as compared with other persons subject to lesser limitations on the same right.

I regret that I do not feel able to agree with this line of reasoning. In my view, when the Court is called on to rule on a breach of the Convention which has been alleged by the applicant and contested by the respondent Government, it is the Court's duty, provided that the application is admissible, to decide the point by giving an answer on the merits of the issue that has been raised. The Court cannot escape this responsibility by employing formulas that are liable to limit excessively the scope of Article 14 to the point of depriving it of all practical values.

Admittedly, there are extreme situations where an existing difference of treatment is so minimal that it entails no real prejudice, physical or moral, for the persons concerned. In that event, no discrimination within the meaning of Article 14 could be discerned, even if on occasions it might be difficult to produce an objective and rational explanation for the difference of treatment. It is only in such conditions that, in my opinion, the maxim *de minimis non curat praetor* would be admissible (see, *mutatis mutandis*, my separate opinion appended to the Marckx judgment, p. 58). I do not, however, find these conditions satisfied in the present case, with the result that a definite position must be taken regarding the alleged violation of Article 14 in relation to the complaints made by the applicant.

(a) The diversity of domestic laws, which is characteristic of a federal State, can in itself never constitute a discrimination, and there is no necessity to justify diversity of this kind. To claim the contrary would be to disregard totally the very essence of federalism.

(c) and (d) The difference of character between homosexual conduct and heterosexual conduct seems obvious, and the moral and social problems to which they give rise are not at all the same. Similarly there exists a genuine difference, of character as well as of degree between the moral and social problems raised by the two forms of homosexuality, male and female. The differing treatment given to them under the criminal law is thus founded, to my mind, on clearly objective justifications.

Accordingly, I come to the conclusion that there has been no breach of Article 14 read in conjunction with Article 8 in respect of any of the heads of complaint relied on by the applicant.

DISSENTING OPINION OF JUDGE PINHEIRO FARINHA
(Translation)

I am unable to agree with the views and conclusions expressed in the present case by my eminent colleagues as regards the breach by the United Kingdom of Article 3 of the Convention.

In my opinion, there was no victim and the Court does not have jurisdiction to take cognisance of a breach alleged by someone who is not a victim.

The action by the police was decided on (paragraph 33) in implementation of the Misuse of Drugs Act 1971 and not with a view to taking action under the criminal law against homosexuality.

The police investigation 'took place in the context of a more extensive operation on the part of the police, the object of which was to trace a minor who was missing from home and believed to be associating with homosexuals' (dissenting opinion of Judge Matscher) and it did not lead to any criminal prosecution being brought (paragraph 41).

The file on the case was closed by the prosecuting authorities, despite the fact that the applicant was the secretary of an organisation campaigning for the legalisation of homosexuality and notwithstanding the proof of his homosexual tendencies.

I come to the conclusion that because the legislation was not enforced against him and is applicable not directly but only after a concrete decision by the authorities, the applicant was not a victim.

There being no victim, the conclusion must be that there was no breach of Article 8 or of Article 14 taken together with Article 8.

I would further emphasise that 'there can be no denial that some degree of regulation of male homosexual conduct, as indeed of other forms of sexual conduct, can be justified as 'necessary in a democratic society', and that 'this necessity for some degree of control may even extend to consensual acts committed in private' (paragraph 49).

PARTIALLY DISSENTING OPINION OF JUDGE WALSH

Is the applicant a 'victim' within the meaning of Article 25?

1. The law of Northern Ireland does not make homosexuality a crime nor does it make all homosexual activities criminal. The 1885 Act is the only one of the two legislative provisions attacked by these present proceedings that can be described as dealing solely with homosexual activities. The Act of 1885 makes criminal the commission of acts of gross indecency between male persons whether in private or public. The provisions of the Act of 1861 which is also impugned by the applicant applies equally to heterosexual activities and homosexual activities. The applicant's complaint is directed only towards the application of the provision of the 1861 Act to homosexual activities of the type mentioned in the section impugned. Of these the Court is in

reality concerned with but one, namely sodomy between male persons.

2. The Act of 1885 does not specifically designate any particular acts of gross indecency but simply prohibits 'gross indecency'. Acts of indecency between male persons are not *per se* criminal offences but only such of them as amount to gross indecency'. What particular acts in any given case may be held to amount to 'gross indecency' is a matter for the court, which means in effect the jury, to decide on the particular facts of each case.

3. The applicant did not claim that he had at any time indulged in any of the activities prohibited either by the law of 1861 or by the law of 1885, nor has he stated that he desires to indulge in them or that he intends to do so. In effect his case is that if he should choose to engage in any of the prohibited activities the effect of the law, if enforced, would be to violate the protection of his private life which is guaranteed by Article 8 of the Convention. In fact no action has been taken against him by the authorities under either of the legislative provisions referred to.

4. It is true that the police displayed an interest in the question of whether or not he had indulged in homosexual activities. It is not known to the Court whether or not the activities in question constituted offences under either of the impugned legislative provisions. The documentary material which gave rise to this police interest came to light during the execution by the police of a search warrant issued pursuant to the laws which prohibit the misuse of drugs. The applicant was requested to accompany the police to the police station for the purpose, *inter alia*, of continuing inquiries into his suspected homosexual activities. The applicant voluntarily agreed to go to the police station. If he had been brought there against his will solely for the purpose of being interrogated about his alleged homosexual activities, he would have been the victim of false imprisonment and under the law of Northern Ireland he would have had an action for damages in the ordinary civil courts. So far as is disclosed by the evidence in the application, no such action has ever been brought or contemplated and it has not been suggested that the applicant's visit to the police station was other than

purely voluntary. It is common case that at the police station he was informed by the police that he was under no obligation to answer any questions or to make any statement. Notwithstanding this, the applicant voluntarily made a statement the contents of which have not been disclosed to the Court. The Court does not know whether the statement was incriminatory or exculpatory. No prosecution was ever instituted against the applicant either by the police or by the Director of Public Prosecutions in respect of any alleged illegal homosexual activities.

No question of the privacy of the applicant's home being invaded arises as the entry to his house was carried out under a valid search warrant dealing with the abuse of drugs and no complaint has been made about the warrant or the entry. Some personal papers, including correspondence and diaries belonging to the applicant in which were described homosexual activities, were taken away by the police. The Court has not been informed whether the papers were irrelevant to the suspected drug offences being investigated and in respect of which there has been no complaint.

5. It is clear that the applicant's case is more in the nature of a 'class action'. In so far as he is personally concerned, it scarcely amounts to a *quia timet* action. Having suffered no prosecution himself he is in effect asking the Court to strike down two legislative provisions of a member state. The Court has no jurisdiction of a declaratory character in this area unrelated to an injury actually suffered or alleged to have been suffered by the applicant. In my view, if the Court were to undertake any such competence in cases where the applicant has neither been a victim nor is imminently to be a victim, the consequences would be far-reaching in every member state.

6. In my opinion the applicant has not established that he is a victim within the meaning of Article 25 of the Convention and he is therefore not entitled to the ruling he seeks.

ALLEGED BREACH OF ARTICLE 8

7. If the applicant is to be regarded as being a victim within the meaning of Article 25, then the applicability of Article 8 to his case falls to be considered.

Paragraph 1 of Article 8 provides that 'everyone has the right to respect for his private and family life, his home and his correspondence'. There is no suggestion that any point relating to family life arises in this case. Therefore the complaint is in reality one to a claim of right to indulge in any homosexual activities in the course of his private life and, presumably, in private.

8. The first matter to consider is the meaning of paragraph 1 of Article 8. Perhaps the best and most succinct legal definition of privacy is that given by Warren and Brandeis — it is 'the right to be let alone'. The question is whether under Article 8 § 1, the right to respect for one's private life is to be construed as being an absolute right irrespective of the nature of the activity which is carried on as part of the private life and no interference with this right under any circumstances is permitted save within the terms of paragraph 2 of Article 8. This appears to be the interpretation put upon it by the Court in its judgment.

It is not essentially different to describe the 'private life' protected by Article 8 § 1 as being confined to the private manifestation of the human personality. In any given case the human personality in question may in private life manifest dangerous or errant tendencies calculated to produce ill-effects upon himself or upon others. The Court does not appear to consider as a material factor that the manifestation in question may involve more than one person participation provided the manifestation can be characterised as an act of private life. If for the purposes of this case this assumption is to be accepted, one proceeds to the question of whether or not the interference complained of can be justified under paragraph 2. This in turn begs the question that under Article 8 the inseparable social dimensions of private life or 'private morality' are limited to the confines of paragraph 2 of Article 8. It is beyond question that the interference, if there was such, was in accordance with the law. The question posed by paragraph 2 is whether the interference permitted by the law is necessary in a democratic society in the interests of the protection of health or morals or the rights and freedoms of others.

9. This raises the age-old philosophical question of what the

purpose of law is. Is there a realm of morality which is not the law's business or is the law properly concerned with moral principles? In the context of United Kingdom jurisprudence and the true philosophy of law this debate in modern times has been between Professor H. L. A. Hart and Lord Devlin. Generally speaking the former accepts the philosophy propounded in the last century by John Stuart Mill while the latter contends that morality is properly the concern of the law. Lord Devlin argues that as the law exists for the protection of society it must not only protect the individual from injury, corruption and exploitation but it

> must protect also the institutions and the community of ideas, political and moral, without which people cannot live together. Society cannot ignore the morality of the individual any more than it can his loyalty; it flourishes on both and without either, it dies.

He claims that the criminal law of England not only 'has from the very first concerned itself with moral principles but continues to concern itself with moral principles.' Among the offences which he pointed to as having been brought within the criminal law on the basis of moral principle, notwithstanding that it could be argued that they do not endanger the public, were euthanasia, the killing of another at his own request, suicide pacts, duelling, abortion, incest between brother and sister. These are acts which he viewed as ones which could be done in private and without offence to others and need not involve the corruption or exploitation of others. Yet, as he pointed out, no one has gone so far as to suggest that they should all be left outside the criminal law as matters of private morality.

10. It would appear that the United Kingdom does claim that in principle it can legislate against immorality. In modern United Kingdom legislation a number of penal statutes appear to be based upon moral principles and the function of these penal sanctions is to enforce moral principles. Cruelty to animals is illegal because of a moral condemnation of enjoyment derived from the infliction of pain upon sentient creatures. The laws restricting or preventing gambling are concerned with the ethical significance of gambling which is confined to the effect that it

may have on the character of the gambler as a member of society. The legislation against racial discrimination has as its object the shaping of people's moral thinking by legal sanctions and the changing of human behaviour by having the authority to punish.

11. The opposite view, traceable in English jurisprudence to John Stuart Mill, is that the law should not intervene in matters of private moral conduct more than necessary to preserve public order and to protect citizens against what is injurious and offensive and that there is a sphere of moral conduct which is best left to individual conscience just as if it were equitable to liberty of thought or belief. The recommendations of the Wolfenden Committee relied partly upon this view to favour the non-intervention of the law in case of homosexual activities between consenting adult males. On this aspect of the matter the Wolfenden Committee stated,

> There remains one additional counter-argument which we believe to be decisive, namely, the importance which society and the law ought to give to individual freedom of choice in action in matters of private morality. Unless a deliberate attempt is to be made by society, acting through the agency of the law, to equate the sphere of crime with that of sin, there must remain a realm of private morality and immorality which is, in brief and crude terms, not the law's business. To say this is not to condone or encourage private immorality.

This aspect of the Wolfenden Committee's report apparently commands itself to the Court (see paragraphs 60 and 61 of the judgment).

12. The Court also agrees with the conclusion in the Wolfenden Report to the effect that there is a necessity for some degree of control even in respect of consensual acts committed in private notably where there is a call 'to provide sufficient safeguards against exploitation and corruption of others, particularly those who are especially vulnerable because they are young, weak in body or mind, inexperienced, or in a state of special physical, official or economic dependence' (paragraph 49 of the judgment). Furthermore, the Court accepts that some form of legislation is necessary to protect not only particular sections

of society but also the moral ethos of society as a whole (ibid.). However, experience has shown that exploitation and corruption of others is not confined to persons who are young, weak in body or mind or inexperienced or in a state of physical, moral or economic dependence.

13. The fact that a person consents to take part in the commission of homosexual acts is not proof that such person is sexually oriented by nature in that direction. A distinction must be drawn between homosexuals who are such because of some kind of innate instinct or pathological constitution judged to be incurable and those whose tendency comes from a lack of normal sexual development or from habit or from experience or from other similar causes but whose tendency is not incurable. So far as the incurable category is concerned, the activities must be regarded as abnormalities or even as handicaps and treated with the compassion and tolerance which is required to prevent those persons from being victimised in respect of tendencies over which they have no control and for which they are not personally responsible. However, other considerations are raised when these tendencies are translated into activities. The corruption for which the Court acknowledges need for control and the protection of the moral ethos of the community referred to by the Court may be closely associated with the translation of such tendencies into activities. Even assuming one of the two persons involved has the incurable tendency, the other may not. It is known that many male persons who are heterosexual or pansexual indulge in these activities not because of any incurable tendency but for sexual excitement. However, it is to be acknowledged that the case for the applicant was argued on the basis of the position of a male person who is by nature homosexually predisposed or orientated. The Court, in the absence of evidence to the contrary, has accepted this as the basis of the applicant's case and in its judgment rules only in respect of males who are so homosexually orientated (see, for example, paragraphs 32, 41 and 60 of the judgment).

14. If it is accepted that the state has a valid interest in the prevention of corruption and in the preservation of the moral ethos of its society, then the State has a right to enact such laws as it may reasonably think necessary to achieve these objects. The

rule of law itself depends on a moral consensus in the community and in a democracy the law cannot afford to ignore the moral consensus of the community, whether by being either too far below it or too far above it, the law is brought into contempt. Virtue cannot be legislated into existence but non-virtue can be if the legislation renders excessively difficult the struggle after virtue. Such a situation can have an eroding effect on the moral ethos of the community in question. The ultimate justification of law is that it serves moral ends. It is true that many forms of immorality which can have a corrupting effect are not the subject of prohibition or penal legislation. However such omissions do not imply a denial of the possibility of corruption or of the erosion of the moral ethos of the community but acknowledge the practical impossibility of legislating effectively for every area of immorality. Where such legislation is enacted it is a reflection of the concern of the 'prudent legislator'.

Moreover, it must not be overlooked that much of the basis of the Wolfenden Committee's recommendation that homosexual relations between adult males should be decriminalised was the belief that the law was difficult to enforce and that when enforced was likely to do more harm than good by encouraging other evils such as blackmail. This is obviously not necessarily of universal validity. The relevant conditions may vary from one community to another. Experience also shows that certain sexual activities which are not in themselves contraventions of the criminal law can also be fruitful subjects for blackmail when they offend the moral ethos of the community, e.g. adultery, female homosexuality and, even, where it is not illegal, male homosexuality.

15. Sexual morality is only one part of the total area of morality and a question which cannot be avoided is whether sexual morality is 'only private morality' or whether it has an inseparable social dimension. Sexual behaviour is determined more by cultural influence than by instinctive needs. Cultural trends and expectations can create drives mistakenly thought to be intrinsic instinctual urges. The legal arrangement and prescriptions set up to regulate sexual behaviour are very important formative factors in the shaping of cultural and social institutions.

16. In my view, the Court's reference to the fact that in most countries in the Council of Europe homosexual acts in private between adults are no longer criminal (paragraph 60 of the judgment) does not really advance the argument. The twenty-one countries making up the Council of Europe extend geographically from Turkey to Iceland and from the Mediterranean to the Arctic Circle and encompass considerable diversities of culture and moral values. The Court states that it cannot overlook the marked changes which have occurred in the laws regarding homosexual behaviour throughout the member states (ibid.) It would be unfortunate if this should lead to the erroneous inference that a Euro-norm in the law concerning homosexual practices has been or can be evolved.

17. Religious beliefs in Northern Ireland are very firmly held and directly influence the views and outlook of the vast majority of persons in Northern Ireland on questions of sexual morality. In so far as male homosexuality is concerned, and in particular sodomy, this attitude to sexual morality may appear to set the people of Northern Ireland apart from many people in other communities in Europe, but whether that fact constitutes a failing is, to say the least, debatable. Such views on unnatural sexual practices do not differ materially from those which throughout history conditioned the moral ethos of the Jewish, Christian and Muslim cultures.

18. The criminal law at no time has been uniform throughout the several legal systems within the United Kingdom. The Court recognises that where there are disparate cultural communities residing within the same state it may well be that different requirements, both moral and social, will face the governing authorities (paragraph 56 of the judgment). The Court also recognises that the contested measures must be seen in the context of Northern Ireland society (ibid.). The United Kingdom Government, having responsibility for statutory changes in any of the legal systems which operate within the United Kingdom, sounded out opinion in Northern Ireland on this question of changing the law in respect of homosexual offences. While it is possible that the United Kingdom Government may have been mistaken

in its assessment of the effect the sought-after change in the law would have on the community in Northern Ireland, nevertheless it is in as good, if not a better; position than is the Court to assess that situation. Criminal sanctions may not be the most desirable way of dealing with the situation but again that has to be assessed in light of the conditions actually prevailing in Northern Ireland. In all cultures, matters of sexual morality are particularly sensitive ones and the effects of certain forms of sexual immorality are not susceptible of the same precise objective assessment that is possible in matters such as torture or degrading and inhuman treatment. To that extent the Court's reference in its judgment (paragraph 60) to Tyrer's case is not really persuasive in the present case. It is respectfully suggested that the Marckx judgment is not really relevant in the present case as that concerned the position of an illegitimate child whose own actions were not in any way in question.

19. Even if it should be thought, and I do not so think, that the people of Northern Ireland are more 'backward' than the other societies within the Council of Europe because of their attitude towards homosexual practices, that is very much a value judgment which depends totally upon the initial premise. It is difficult to gauge what would be the effect on society in Northern Ireland if the law were now to permit (even with safeguards for young people and people in need of protection) homosexual practices of the type at present forbidden by law. I venture the view that the Government concerned, having examined the position, is in a better position to evaluate that than this Court, particularly as the Court admits the competence of the State to legislate in this matter but queries the proportionality of the consequences of the legislation in force.

20. The law has a role in influencing moral attitudes and if the respondent Government is of the opinion that the change sought in the legislation would have a damaging effect on moral attitudes then in my view it is entitled to maintain the legislation it has. The judgment of the Court does not constitute a declaration to the effect that the particular homosexual practices which are subject to penalty by the legislation in question virtually amount

to fundamental human rights. However, that will not prevent it being hailed as such by those who seek to blur the essential difference between homosexual and heterosexual activities.

21. Even the Wolfenden Report felt that one of the functions of criminal law was to preserve public order and decency and to provide sufficient safeguards against the exploitation and corruption of others and therefore recommended that it should continue to be an offence 'for a third party to procure or attempt to procure an act of gross indecency between male persons whether or not the act to be procured constitutes a criminal offence.' Adults, even consenting adults, can be corrupted and may be exploited by reason of their own weaknesses. In my view this is an area in which the legislature has a wide discretion or margin of appreciation which should not be encroached upon save where it is clear beyond doubt that the legislation is such that no reasonable community could enact. In my view no such proof has been established in this case.

22. In the United States of America there has been considerable litigation concerning the question of privacy and the guarantees as to privacy enshrined in the Constitution of the United States. The United States Supreme Court and other United States courts have upheld the right of privacy of married couples against legislation which sought to control sexual activities within marriage, including sodomy. However, these courts have refused to extend the constitutional guarantee of privacy which is available to married couples to homosexual activities or to heterosexual sodomy outside marriage. The effect of this is that the public policy upholds as virtually absolute, privacy within marriage and privacy of sexual activity within marriage.

It is a valid approach to hold that, as the family is the fundamental unit group of society, the interests of marital privacy would normally be superior to the state's interest in the pursuit of certain sexual activities which would in themselves be regarded as immoral and calculated to corrupt. Outside marriage there is no such compelling interest of privacy which by its nature ought to prevail in respect of such activities.

23. It is to be noted that Article 8 § 1 of the Convention speaks of 'private and family life'. If the *ejusdem generis* rule is to

be applied, then the provision should be interpreted as relating to private life in that context as, for example, the right to raise one's children according to one's own philosophical and religious tenets and generally to pursue without interference the activities which are akin to those pursued in the privacy of family life and such as are in the course of ordinary human and fundamental rights. No such claim can be made for homosexual practices.

24. In my opinion there has been no breach of Article 8 of the Convention.

25. I agree with the judgment of the Court in respect of Article 14.

EUROPEAN COURT OF HUMAN RIGHTS

In the Norris case*,

* Note by the registry: The case is numbered 6/1987/129/180. The second figure indicates the year in which the case was referred to Court and the first figure its place on the list of cases referred to that year; the last two figures indicate, respectively, the case order on the list of cases and of originating applications (to the Commission) referred to the Court since its creation.

The European Court of Human Rights, taking its decision in plenary session pursuant to Rule 50 of the Rules of Court and composed of the following judges :

Mr R. Ryssdal, President,
Mr J. Cremona,
Mr Thór Vilhjálmsson,
Mr F. Gölcüklü,
Mr F. Matscher,
Mr L. -E. Pettiti,
Mr B. Walsh,
Sir Vincent Evans,
Mr C. Russo,
Mr R. Bernhardt,
Mr A. Spielmann,
Mr J. De Meyer,
Mr J. A. Carrillo Salcedo,
Mr N. Valticos,

and also of Mr M. A. Eissen, Registrar, and Mr H. Petzold, Deputy Registrar.

Having deliberated in private on April 29 and September 29, 1988, delivers the following judgment, which was adopted on the last-mentioned date.

PROCEDURE

1. The case was referred to the Court by the European Commission of Human Rights ('the Commission') on May 14, 1987, within the three-month period laid down in Article 32 para. 1 and Article 47 of the Convention for the Protection of Human Rights and Fundamental Freedoms ('the Convention').

It originated in an application (no. 10581/83) against Ireland lodged with the Commission under Article 25 by Mr David Norris, an Irish citizen, on October 5, 1983.

The Commission's request referred to Articles 44 and 48 of the Convention and to the declaration whereby Ireland recognised the compulsory jurisdiction of the Court (Article 46). It sought a decision from the Court as to whether the facts of the case disclosed a breach by the respondent State of its obligations under Article 8 of the Convention.

2. In response to the enquiry made in accordance with Rule 33 para. 3 (d) of the Rules of Court, the applicant stated that he wished to take part in the proceedings pending before the Court and designated the lawyer who would represent him (Rule 30).

3. The Chamber to be constituted included *ex officio* Mr B. Walsh the elected Judge of Irish nationality (Article 43 of the Convention and Mr R. Ryssdal, the President of the Court (Rule 21 para. 3 (b)). On May 23, 1987, in the presence of the Registrar, the President drew by lot the names of the other five members, namely Mr Thór Vilhjálmsson, Mr G. Lagergren, Mr F. Matscher, Mr J. Q. Pinheiro Farinha and Mr R. Bernhardt (Article 43 in fine of the Convention and Rule 21 para. 4).

4. Mr Ryssdal, who had assumed the office of President of the Chamber (Rule 21 para. 5), consulted, through the Registrar, the —(?) of the Irish Government ('the Government'), the delegate of the Commission and the lawyer of the applicant on the need for a written procedure (Rule 37 para. 1). In accordance with his orders, the following documents were received by the registry:

- the Government's memorial, on October 26, 1987 ;
- the applicant's memorial, on November 2, 1987 ;
- supplementary memorial by the government, on April 25, 1988.

In a letter received by the Registrar on December 11, 1987, the Secretary to the Commission indicated that the delegate would submit her observations at the hearing.

5. On November 30, 1987, the Chamber decided to relinquish jurisdiction in favour of the plenary Court (Rule 50).

6. Having consulted — through the Registrar — those who would be appearing before the Court, the President directed on

December 16, 1987 that the oral proceedings should commence on April 25, 1988 (Rule 38).

7. The hearing took place in public in the Human Rights Building, Strasbourg, on the appointed day. The Court had held a preparatory meeting immediately beforehand.

There appeared before the Court:

(a) for the Government
Mr P. E. Smyth — Agent
Mr E. Comyn, Senior Counsel,
Mr D. Gleeson, Senior Counsel,
Mr J. O'Reilly, Barrister-at-Law, — Counsel
Mr J. Hamilton, Office of the Attorney General. — Advisor

(b) for the Commission
Mrs G. H. Thune. — Delegate

(c) for the applicant
Senator M. Robinson, Senior Counsel, — Counsel
Mr J. Jay, Solicitor of the Supreme Court. — Advisor

The Court heard addresses by Mrs Thune for the Commission, by Senator Robinson for the applicant and by Mr Comyn and Mr Gleeson for the Government, as well as their replies to its questions.

AS TO THE FACTS

I. THE PARTICULAR CIRCUMSTANCES OF THE CASE

8. Mr David Norris was born in 1944. He is an Irish citizen. He is now, and has been since 1967, a lecturer in English at Trinity College, Dublin. At present he sits in the second chamber (Seanad Eireann) of the Irish Parliament, being one of the three Senators elected by the graduates of Dublin University.

9. Mr Norris is an active homosexual and has been a campaigner for homosexual rights in Ireland since 1971; in 1974 he became a founder member and chairman of the Irish Gay Rights Movement. His complaints are directed against the existence in Ireland of laws which make certain homosexual practices between consenting adult men criminal offences.

10. In November 1977 the applicant instituted proceedings in the High Court (see paragraphs 21-24 below) claiming that

the impugned laws were no longer in force by reason of the effect of Article 50 of the Constitution of Ireland, which declared that laws passed before the Constitution but which were inconsistent with it did not continue to be in force. Evidence was given of the extent to which the applicant had been affected by that legislation and had suffered interference with his right to respect for private life. Salient points in this evidence were summarised as follows:

(i) The applicant gave evidence of having suffered deep depression and loneliness on realising that he was irreversibly homosexual and that any overt expression of his sexuality would expose him to criminal prosecution.

(ii) The applicant claimed that his health had been affected when in 1969 he fainted at a Dublin restaurant and was sent to Baggot Street Hospital for tests which resulted in his being referred to a psychiatrist. He was under the psychiatric care of Dr. McCracken for a period in excess of six months. Dr. McCracken's advise to the applicant was that, if he wished to avoid anxiety attacks of this kind, he should leave Ireland and live in a country where the laws relating to homosexual behaviours had been reformed. Dr. McCracken stated in evidence that the applicant was in a normal condition at time of the first consultation. He did not recall being made aware of a history of collapse.

(iii) No attempt had been made to institute a prosecution against the applicant or the organisation of which the applicant was then the chairman (see paragraph 9 above). The applicant informed the police authorities of his organisation's activities but met with a sympathetic response and was never subjected to police questioning.

(iv) The applicant had participated in a television programme on RTE, the state broadcasting company, in or about July 1975. The programme consisted of an interview with him in the course of which he admitted to being a homosexual but denied that this was an illness and that it would prevent him from functioning as a normal member of society. A complaint was lodged against that programme. The Broadcasting Complaints Advisory Committee's report referred to the existing law criminalising homosexual activity and upheld the complaint on the ground that the programme was in breach of the Current/Public Affairs Broadcasting Code in that it could be interpreted as advocacy of homosexual practices.

(v) The applicant gave evidence of suffering verbal abuse and threats of violence subsequent to the interview with him on RTE, which he attributed in some degree to the criminalising of homosexual activity. He also alleged in evidence that in the past his mail was opened by the postal authorities.

(vi) The applicant admitted to having a physical relationship with another man and that he feared that he or the person with whom he had the relationship, who normally lived outside Ireland, could face prosecution.

(vii) The applicant also claimed to have suffered what Mr Justice Henchy in a dissenting judgment in the Supreme Court (see paragraph 22 below) alluded to as follows:

... fear of prosecution or of social obloquy has restricted him in his social and other relations with male colleagues and friends: and in a number of subtle but insidiously intrusive and wounding ways he has been restricted in or thwarted from engaging in activities which heterosexuals take for granted as aspects of the necessary expression of their human personality and as ordinary incidents of their citizenship.

11. It is common ground that at no time before or since the court proceedings brought by the applicant has he been charged with any offence in relation to his admitted homosexual activities. However he remains legally at risk of being so prosecuted, either by the Director of Public Prosecutions or by way of a private prosecution initiated by a common informer up to the stage of return for trial (see paragraphs 15-19 below).

II. THE RELEVANT LAW IN IRELAND

A. THE IMPUGNED STATUTORY PROVISIONS

12. Irish law does not make homosexuality such a crime. But certain statutory provisions in force in Ireland penalise certain homosexual activities. Some of these are penalised by the Offences against the Person Act, 1861 ('the 1861 Act') and the Criminal Law Amendment Act, 1885 ('the 1885 Act').

The provisions relevant to the present case are Sections 61 and 62 of the 1861 Act. Section 61 of the 1861 Act, as amended in 1892, provides that:

> Whosoever shall be convicted of the abominable crime of buggery, committed either with mankind or with any animal, shall be liable to be kept in penal servitude for life.

Section 62 of the 1861 Act, as similarly amended, provides that:

> Whosoever shall attempt to commit the said abominable crime, or should be guilty of any assault with intent to commit the same, or of any indecent assault upon a male person, shall be guilty of a misdemeanour, and being convicted thereof shall be liable to be kept in penal servitude for any term not exceeding ten years.

The offences of buggery or of an attempt to commit the same may be committed by male or female persons.

Section 11 of the 1885 Act deals only with male persons. It provides that:

> Any male person who, in public or in private, commits, or is a party to the commission of, or procures or attempts to procure the commission by any male person of, any act of gross indecency with another male person, shall be guilty of a misdemeanour, and being convicted thereof shall be liable at the discretion of the court to be imprisoned for any term not exceeding two years, with or without hard labour.

13. Sections 61 and 62 of the 1861 Act should be read in conjunction with the provisions of the Penal Servitude Act 1891, Section 1, by virtue of which the court is empowered to

impose a lesser sentence of penal servitude than that mentioned in the 1861 or, in lieu thereof, a sentence of imprisonment for a term not exceeding two years or a fine. The provisions of the 1861 Act and the 1885 Act are also subject to the power given to the court by Section 1(2) of the Probation of Offenders Act 1907, to apply, by way of substitution, certain more lenient measures.

The terms 'hard labour' and 'penal servitude' no longer have any practical significance, since anyone now sentenced to 'hard labour' or 'penal servitude' will, in practice, serve an ordinary prison sentence.

14. The 1885 Act is the only one of the legislative provisions attacked in the instant case that can be described as dealing solely with homosexual activities. What particular acts in any given case may be held to amount to gross indecency is a matter which is not statutorily defined and is therefore for the courts to decide on the particular facts of each case.

B. THE ENFORCEMENT OF THE RELEVANT STATUTORY PROVISIONS

15. The right to prosecute persons before a court other than a court of summary jurisdiction is governed by Article 30, Section 3 of the Constitution which is as follows:

> All crimes and offences prosecuted in any court constituted under Article 34 of this Constitution other than a court of summary jurisdiction shall be prosecuted in the name of the People and at the suit of the Attorney General or some other person authorised in accordance with law to act for that purpose.

Section 9 of the Criminal Justice (Administration) Act, 1924, as adapted by the Constitution (Consequential Provisions) Act, 1937, provides that:

> All criminal charges prosecuted upon indictment in any court shall be prosecuted at the suit of the Attorney General of Ireland.

16. The provisions of the Prosecution of Offences Act 1974 extended to the Director of Public Prosecutions most of the prosecuting functions exercised by the Attorney General. The

Director of Public Prosecutions (an office created by that Act) is independent of the Government and a permanent official in the Civil Service of the state as distinct from the Civil Service of the Government.

17. Any member of the public, whether an Irish citizen or not, has the right as a 'common informer' to bring a private prosecution. He need not have any direct interest in the alleged offence or be personally affected by it. A private prosecutor's rights are limited in respect of offences which are not triable summarily. In The State (Ennis) v. Farrell [1966] Irish Reports 107, it was held by the Supreme Court that the effect of Section 9 of the Criminal Justice (Administration) Act 1924 was that a private prosecutor may conduct prosecution up to the point where the judge of the District Court decides that the evidence is sufficient to warrant a committal for trial in cases of indictable offences i.e. triable with a jury. Thereafter the Attorney General, or now also the Director of Public Prosecutions, becomes *dominus litis* and must then consider whether or not he should present an indictment against the accused who has been returned by the District Court for trial with a jury.

18. The offences which are at issue in the present case, namely those set out in Sections 61 and 62 of the 1861 Act and in Section 11 of the 1885 Act, are indictable offences. Indictable offences are only triable summarily in the District Court if the judge of the District Court is of the opinion that the facts constitute a minor offence and the accused, on being informed of his right to trial by jury, expressly waives that right. This availability of summary trial is provided for by the Criminal Justice Act, 1951 and is limited to those indictable offences set out in the Schedule to that Act. This does not include the offences under Sections 61 and 62 of the 1861 Act. The summary trial procedure is available in respect of a offence under Section 11 of the 1885 Act where the accused is over the age of sixteen years and the person with whom the act is alleged to have been committed is legally unable to consent for being under the age of sixteen years or an idiot, an imbecile or a feeble-minded person. Thus a summary trial can never be had in cases involving consenting adults and, save where the

accused pleads guilty, the case can be heard only with a jury whether the prosecution was commenced by a private prosecutor or by the Director of Public Prosecutions.

Moreover, the Criminal Procedure Act 1967 permits a person charged with any indictable offence (save an offence under the Treason Act, 1939), murder, attempt to murder, conspiracy to murder, piracy or an offence under Section 3(1)(i) of the Geneva Conventions Act, 1962 to plead guilty in the District Court. If the Director of Public Prosecutions, or the Attorney General, as the case may be, consents, the case may be disposed off summarily in that Court. If sentence is imposed by the District Court, it cannot exceed twelve months' imprisonment. If the judge of the District Court is of the opinion that the offence warrants a greater penalty, he may send the accused forward to the Circuit Court for sentence. In such a case an accused may change his plea to one of not guilty and the case will then be tried with a jury. The Circuit Court has a discretion to impose a sentence up to the limits permitted by the relevant statutory provision.

19. Therefore, while a private prosecution may be initiated by common informer, a prosecution brought under one of the impugned provisions cannot proceed to trial before a jury unless an indictment is laid by the Director of Public Prosecutions. According to the Office of the Director of Public Prosecutions there have not been private prosecutions arising out of the homosexual activity in private of consenting male adults since the inception of the Office in 1974.

20. The following statement was made by the Office of the Director of Public Prosecutions in September 1984, in reply to a question as by the Commission:

> The Director has no stated prosecution policy on any branch of the criminal law. He has no unstated policy not to enforce any offence. Each case is treated on its merits.

The Government's statistics show that no public prosecutions, in respect of homosexual activities, were brought during the relevant period except where minors were involved or the acts were committed in public or without consent.

III. THE PROCEEDINGS BEFORE THE NATIONAL COURTS

21. In November 1977 the applicant brought proceedings in the Irish High Court seeking a declaration that Sections 61 and 62 of the 1861 Act and Section 11 of the 1885 Act were not continued in force since the enactment of the Constitution of Ireland (see paragraph 1 above) and therefore did not form part of Irish law.

Mr Justice McWilliam, in his judgement of October 10, 1980, found, another facts, that, 'one of the effects of criminal sanctions against homosexual acts is to reinforce the misapprehension and general prejudice of the public and increase the anxiety and guilt feelings of homosexuals leading, on occasions, to depression and the serious consequences which can follow from that unfortunate disease'. However, he dismissed Mr Norris's action on legal grounds.

22. On appeal, the Supreme Court, by a three to two majority decision of April 22, 1983, upheld the judgement of the High Court. Supreme Court was satisfied that the applicant had *locus standi* to bring an action for a declaration even though he had not been prosecuted for any of the offences in question. The majority held that 'as long as the legislation stands and continues to proclaim a criminal, the conduct which the plaintiff asserts he has a right to engage in, such right, if it exists, is threatened, and the plaintiff has standing to seek the protection of the court.'

23. In the course of these proceedings it was contended on behalf of the applicant that the judgement of October 22, 1981 of the European Court of Human Rights in the Dudgeon case (Series A no. 45) should have followed. In support of this plea, it was argued that, since Ireland had ratified the European Convention on Human Rights, there arose a presumption that the Constitution was compatible with the Convention and that, in considering a question as to inconsistency under Article 50 of the Constitution, regard should be had to whether the laws being considered are consistent with the Convention itself.

In rejecting these submissions, Chief Justice O'Higgins, in the majority judgement stated that 'the Convention is an international agreement' which 'does not and cannot form part of [Ireland's] domestic law nor affect in any way questions which arise thereunder.' The Chief Justice said: 'This is made quite clear by Article 29, Section 6, of the Constitution which declares: 'No international agreement shall be part of the domestic law of the state save as may be determined by the Oireachtas.'

In fact, the European Court of Human Rights already noted in its judgement of July 1, 1961 in the Lawless case (Series A no. 3, pp. 40-41, para. 25) that the Oireachtas had not introduced legislation to make the Convention on Human Rights part of the municipal law of Ireland.

24. The Supreme Court considered the laws making homosexual conduct criminal to be consistent with the Constitution and that no right of privacy encompassing consensual homosexual activity could be derived from the Christian and democratic nature of the Irish State so as to prevail against the operation of such sanctions. In its majority decision, the Supreme Court based itself, *inter alia,* on the following considerations:

(1) Homosexuality has always been condemned in Christian teachings as being morally wrong. It has equally been regarded by society for many centuries as an offence against nature and a very serious crime.

(2) Exclusive homosexuality, whether the condition be congenital or acquired, can result in great distress and unhappiness for the individual and can lead to depression, despair and suicide.

(3) The homosexually oriented can be importuned into a homosexual lifestyle which can become habitual.

(4) Male homosexual conduct has resulted, in other countries, in the spread of all forms of venereal disease and this has now become a significant public health problem in England.

(5) Homosexual conduct can be inimical to marriage and is *per se* harmful to it as an institution.

The Supreme Court, however, awarded the applicant his costs, both of the proceedings before the High Court and of the appeal to the Supreme Court.

PROCEEDINGS BEFORE THE COMMISSION

25. Mr Norris applied to the Commission on October 5, 1983 (application no. 10581/83). He complained of the existence in Ireland of legislation which prohibits male homosexual activity (Sections 61 and 62 of the 1861 Act and Section 11 of the 1885 Act). Mr Norris alleged that the prohibition on male homosexual activity constitute continuing interference with his right to respect for private life (including sexual life), contrary to Article 8 of the Convention. The National Gay Federation joined with the applicant the application to the Commission and both made other claims under Articles 1 and 13 of the Convention.

26. By decision of May 16, 1985, the Commission declared the application admissible in respect of the alleged interference with Mr Norris's private life. The claims made under Articles 1 and 13 were declared inadmissible, as were the aforesaid Federation's entire complaints.

In its report adopted on March 12, 1987 (Article 31 of the Convention), the Commission expressed the opinion, by six votes to five that there had been a violation of Article 8 of the Convention.

The full text of the Commission's opinion and the joint dissenting opinion contained in the report is reproduced as an annexe to this judgment.

FINAL SUBMISSIONS MADE TO THE COURT

27. At the hearing, the Government maintained the final submission in their memorial of October 23, 1987, in which they requested the Court:

(1) to decide and declare that the applicant is not a 'victim' with the meaning of Article 25 of the European Convention on Human Rights and therefore that there has been no breach of the Convention in this case; or, in the alternative

(2) to decide and declare that the present laws in Ireland relating to homosexual acts do not give rise to a breach of Article 8 of the Convention in that the laws are necessary in a democratic society for the protection of morals and for the protection of the rights of others

> for the purposes of paragraph 2 of Article of the Convention.

AS TO THE LAW

I. Whether the applicant is entitled to claim to be a victim under Article 25 para. 1

28. The Government asked the Court, and had made the same plea before the Commission to hold that the applicant could not claim to be a 'victim' within the meaning of Article 25 para. 1 of the Convention which, so far as is relevant, provides that:

> The Commission may receive petitions...from any person... claiming to be the victim of a violation by one of the High Contracting Parties of the rights set forth in [the] Convention ...

The Government submitted that, since the legislation complained of laws never been enforced against the applicant (see paragraphs 11-14 above), his claim was more in the nature of an *actio popularis* by means of which he sought a review in *abstracto* of the contested legislation in the light of the Convention.

29. The Commission considered that Mr Norris could claim to be a victim. In this connection, it referred to certain earlier decisions of the Court, namely the Klass and Others judgment of September 6, 1978, the Marckx judgment of June 13, 1979 and the Dudgeon case judgment of October 22, 1981 (Series A. nos. 28, 31 and 45).

In the Commission's view, although the applicant has not been prosecuted or subjected to any criminal investigation because he is predisposed to commit prohibited sexual acts with consenting adult men by reasons of his homosexual orientation.

30. The Court recalls that, whilst Article 24 of the Convention permits a contracting state to refer to the Commission 'an alleged breach' of the Convention by another contracting state, Article 25 requires that an individual applicant should be able to claim to be actually affected by the measure of which he complains. Article 25 may not be used to found an action; the nature of an *actio popularis;* nor may it form the basis of a clause made in *abstracto* that a law contravenes the Convention (see the Klass

and Others judgment, previously cited, Series A no. 28, pp. 17-18, para. 33).

31. The Court further agrees with the Government that the conditions governing individual applications under Article 25 of the Convention are not necessarily the same as national criteria relating to *locus standi*. National rules in this respect serve purposes different from those contemplated by Article 25 and, whilst those purposes may sometimes be analogous, they need not always be so (ibid., p.19, para. 36).

Be that as it may, the Court has held that Article 25 of the Convention entitles individuals to contend that a law violates their rights by itself, in the absence of an individual measure of implementation, if they run the risk of being directly affected by (see the Johnston and Others judgment of December 18, 1986, Series A no. 112, p.21, para. 42 and the Marckx judgment, previously cited Series A no. 31, p.13, para. 27).

32. In the Court's view, Mr Norris is in substantially the same position as the applicant in the Dudgeon case, which concerned identical legislation then in force in Northern Ireland. As was heard in that case, 'either [he] respects the law and refrains from engaging even in private and with consenting male partners—in prohibited sexual acts to which he is disposed by reason of his homosexual tendencies, or he commits such acts and thereby becomes liable to criminal prosecution' (Series A no. 45, p. 18, para. 41).

33. Admittedly, it appears that there have been no prosecutions under the Irish legislation in question during the relevant period except where minors were involved or the acts were committed in public or without consent. It may be inferred from this that, at the present time, the risk of prosecution in the applicant's case is minimal. However, there is no stated policy on the part of the prosecuting authorities not to enforce the law in this respect (see paragraph 2 above). A law which remains on the statute book, even though it is not enforced in a particular class of cases for a considerable time may be applied again in such cases at any time, if for example there is a change of policy. The applicant can therefore be said to 'run the risk of being directly affected' by the legislation in question. This conclusion is further

supported by the High Court's judgment of October 10, 1980, in which Mr Justice McWilliam, or the witnesses' evidence, found, *inter alia*, that 'One of the effects of criminal sanctions against homosexual acts is to reinforce the misapprehension and general prejudice of the public and increase the anxiety and guilty feelings of homosexuals leading, on occasions, to depression and the serious consequences which can follow from that unfortunate disease (see paragraph 21 above).

34. On the basis of the foregoing considerations, the Court finalised that the applicant can claim to be the victim of a violation of the Convention within the meaning of Article 25 para. 1.

That being so, the Court does not consider it necessary to examine further the applicant's allegations with regard to, *inter alia*, threats of prosecution, claims of interference with his mail, the upholding of a complaint against a television programme on which he appeared and the evidence he gave before the High Court of Ireland of his psychiatric problems (see paragraph 10 above).

II. THE ALLEGED BREACH OF ARTICLE 8

A. THE EXISTENCE OF AN INTERFERENCE

35. Mr Norris complained that under the law in force in Ireland he is liable to criminal prosecution on account of his homosexual conduct. He alleged that he has thereby suffered, and continues to suffer, an unjustified interference with his right to respect for his private life, in breach of Article 8 which provides that:

1. Everyone has the right to respect for his private and family life, his home and his correspondence.
2. There shall be no interference by a public authority with the exercise of this right except such as is in accordance with the law and is necessary in a democratic society in the interests of national security, public safety or the economic well - being of the country, the prevention of disorder or crime, for the protection of health or morals, or for the protection of the rights and freedom of others.

36. The Commission (at paragraph 55 of its report)

considered that:

> One of the main purposes of penal legislation is to deter the proscribed behaviour, and citizens are deemed to conduct themselves or modify their behaviour, in such a way as not to contravene the criminal law. It cannot be said, therefore, that the applicant run no risk of prosecution or that can wholly ignore the legislation question.

The Commission, therefore, found that the legislation complained of interferes with the applicant's right to respect for his private life guaranteed by Article 8 para. 1 of the Convention, in so far as it prohibits the homosexual activities in question even when committed in private between consenting adult men.

37. The Government, on the other hand, contended that it was not possible to conclude that there had been any lack of respect for the applicant's rights under the Convention. In support of their contention, the Government relied on the fact that the applicant had been able to maintain an active public life side by side with a private life free from any interference on the part of the state or its agents. They further submitted that no derogation from the applicant's fundamental rights occur by virtue of the mere existence of laws restricting homosexual behaviour under pain of legal sanctions.

38. The Court agrees with the Commission that, with regard to the interference with an Article 8 right, the present case is indistinguishable from the Dudgeon case. The laws in question are applied so as to prosecute persons in respect of homosexual acts committed in the circumstances mentioned in the first sentence of paragraph 33. Above all, and quite apart from those circumstances, enforcement of the legislation is a matter for the Director of Public Prosecutions who may not fetter his discretion with regard to each individual case by making a general statement of his policy in advance (see paragraph 20). A prosecution may, in any event, be initiated by a member of the public acting as a common informer (see paragraphs 15-19 above).

It is true that, unlike Mr Dudgeon, Mr Norris was not the subject of any police investigation. However, the Court's finding in the Dudgeon case that there was an interference with the applicant's right to respect for his private life was not dependent upon this additional factor. As was held in that case, 'the maintenance in force of the impugned legislation constitutes a continuing interference with the applicant's right to respect for his private life...within the meaning of Article 8 para. 1. In the personal circumstances of the applicant, the very existence of this legislation continuously, directly affects his private life...' (Series A no. 45, p. 18, par.)

The Court therefore finds that the impugned legislation interferes with Mr Norris's right to respect for his private life under Article 8 para. 1.

B. THE EXISTENCE OF A JUSTIFICATION FOR THE INTERFERENCE

39. The interference found by the Court does not satisfy the conditions of paragraph 2 of Article 8 unless it is 'in accordance with the law', has an aim which is legitimate under this paragraph and is 'necessary in a democratic society', for the aforesaid aim (see, as the most recent authority, the Olsson judgment of March 24, 1988, Series A no. 130, p. 29, para. 59).

40. It is common ground that the first two conditions are satisfied. As the Commission pointed out in paragraph 58 of its report, the interference is plainly 'in accordance with the law' since it arises from the very existence of the impugned legislation. Neither was it contested that the interference has a legitimate aim namely the protection of morals.

41. It remains to be determined whether the maintenance in force of the impugned legislation is 'necessary in a democratic society' of the aforesaid aim. According to the Court's case-law, this will not be so unless, *inter alia,* the interference in question answers a pressing social need and in particular is proportionate to the legitimate aim pursued (see, amongst many other authorities, the above-mentioned Olsson judgment, Series A no. 130, p. 31, para. 67).

42. In this respect, the Commission again was of the opinion that the present case was indistinguishable from that of Mr Dudgeon's. At paragraph 62 of its report, it quoted extensively

from those paragraphs of the Dudgeon judgment (paragraphs 48 - 63) in which this question was discussed. In that judgment it was accepted that, since "some form of legislation is 'necessary' to protect particular sections of society as well as the moral ethos of society as a whole, the question in the present case is whether the contested provisions of the law...and their enforcement remain within the bounds of what, in a democratic society, may be regarded as necessary in order to accomplish those aims" (Series A no. 45, p. 21, para. 49).

It was not contended before the Commission that there is a large body of opinion in Ireland which is hostile or intolerant towards homosexual acts committed in private between consenting adults. Nor was it argued that Irish society had a special need to be protected from such activity. In these circumstances, the Commission concluded that the restriction imposed on the applicant under Irish law, by reason of its breadth and absolute character, is disproportionate to the aims sought to be achieved and therefore is not necessary for the reasons laid down in Article 8 para. 2 of the Convention.

43. At the oral hearing, the Government argued that, whilst the criteria of pressing social need and proportionality were valid yardsticks for testing restrictions imposed in the interests of national security, public order or the protection of public health, they could not be applied to determine whether an interference is 'necessary in a democratic society' for the protection of morals; and that further a wider view of necessity should be taken in an area in which the contracting states enjoy a wide margin of appreciation.

In the Government's opinion, the application of these criteria empty the 'moral exception' of meaning. In their view, the identification of 'necessity' with 'pressing social need' in the context of moral values is too restrictive and produces a distorting result, while the test of proportionality involves the evaluation of a moral issue and this is something that the Court should avoid if possible. Within broad parameters, the moral fibre of a democratic nation is a matter for its own institutions and the Government should be allowed a degree of tolerance in their compliance with Article 8, that is to say, a margin of appreciation that would allow the democratic legislature to deal with this problem in the manner which it sees best.

44. The Court is not convinced by this line of argument. As early as 1976, the Court declared in its Handyside judgment of December 7, 1976 that, in investigating whether the protection of morals necessitated the various measures taken, it had to make an assessment of the reality of the pressing social need implied by the notion of 'necessity' in this context and stated that "every 'restriction' imposed in this sphere must be proportionate to the legitimate aim pursued" (Series A no. 24, pp. 21-23, paras. 46, 48, 49). It confirmed this approach in its Dudgeon judgment (Series A no. 45, pp. 20-22, paras. 48 et seq.).

The more recent case of Muller and Others demonstrates that, in the context of the protection of morals, the Court continues to apply the same tests for determining what is 'necessary in a democratic society'. In that case, the Court, in reaching its decision, examines whether the contested measures, which pursued the legitimate aim of protecting morals, both answered a pressing social need and complied with the principle of proportionality (see the judgment of May 24, 1988, Series A no. 133, pp. 21-23, paras. 31-37 and pp. 24 - 2 paras, 40-44).

The Court sees no reason to depart from the approach which emerges from its settled case-law and, although of the three aforementioned judgments, two related to Article 10 of the Convention, it sees no cause to apply different criteria in the context of Article 8.

45. Moreover, in making their submission that the definition of 'necessity' should be given a wider interpretation, the Government in effect put forward no viable tests of their own to replace or complement those mentioned above. The Government's contention would therefore appear to be that the state's discretion in the field of protection of morals is unfettered.

Whilst national authorities as the Court acknowledges—do enjoy wide margin of appreciation in matters of morals, this is not unlimited. It is for the Court, in this field also, to give a ruling on whether an interference is compatible with the Convention (see the previously cited Handyside judgment, Series A no. 24, p. 23, para. ...)

The Government are in effect saying that the Court is precluded from reviewing Ireland's observance of its obligation not to exceed what is necessary in a democratic society when the contested interference with an Article 8 right is in the interests of the 'protection of morals'. The Court cannot accept such as interpretation. To do so would run counter to the terms of Article 19 of the Convention, under which the Court was set up in order 'to ensure the observance of the engagements undertaken by the High Contracting Parties ....'

46. As in the Dudgeon case :

> ... not only the nature of the aim of the restriction but also the nature of the activities involved will affect the scope of the margin of appreciation. The present case concerns a most intimate aspect of private life. Accordingly, there must exist particularly serious reasons before interferences on the part of public authorities can be legitimate for the purposes of paragraph 2 of Article 8 (Series A no. 45, p. 21, para.)

Yet the Government have adduced no evidence which would point to the existence of factors justifying the retention of the impugned laws which are additional to or are of greater weight than those present in the aforementioned Dudgeon case. At paragraph 60 of its judgment of October 22, 1981 (ibid., pp. 23 - 24), the Court noted that,

> As compared with the era when [the] legislation was enacted, there is now a better understanding, and in consequence an increased tolerance, of homosexual behaviour to the extent that in the great majority of the member states of the Council of Europe it is no longer considered to be necessary or appropriate to treat homosexual practices of the kind now in question as in themselves a matter to which the sanctions of the criminal law should be applied; the Court cannot overlook the marked changes which have occurred in this regard in the domestic law of the member states.

It was clear that 'the authorities [had] refrained in recent years from enforcing the law in respect of private homosexual acts between consenting [adult] males . . capable of valid consent'.

There was no evidence to show that this '[had] been injurious to moral standards in Northern Ireland or that there [had] been any public demand for stricter enforcement of the law'.

Applying the same tests to the present case, the Court considers that as regards Ireland, it cannot be maintained that there is a 'pressing social need' to make such acts criminal offences. On the specific issue of proportionality, the Court is of the opinion that 'such justifications as there are for retaining the law in force unamended are outweighed by the detrimental effects which the very existence of the legislative provisions in question can have on the life of a person of homosexual orientation like the applicant. Although members of the public who regard homosexuality as immoral may be shocked, offended or disturbed by the commission by others of private homosexual acts, this cannot on its own warrant the application of penal sanctions when it is, consenting adults alone who are involved (ibid., p. 24 para. 60)'.

47. The Court therefore finds that the reasons put forward as justifying the interference found are not sufficient to satisfy the requirements of paragraph 2 of Article 8. There is accordingly a breach of that Article 8.

III. THE APPLICATION OF ARTICLE 50

48. Under Article 50 of the Convention:

> If the Court finds that a decision or a measure taken by a legal authority or any other authority of a High Contracting Party is completely or partially in conflict with the obligations arising from the...Convention, and if the internal law of the said Party allow only partial reparation to be made for the consequences of this decision or measure, the decision of the Court shall, if necessary, afford just satisfaction to the injured party.

The applicant seeks compensation for damage and reimbursement of legal costs and expenses.

A. DAMAGE

49. The applicant requested the Court to fix such amount by way of damages as would recognise the extent to which he has suffered from the maintenance in force of the legislation.

The Government submitted that the Court should follow its decision of February 27, 1983 in the Dudgeon case on this point (see Series A no. 59) in which it held that a finding of a breach of Article 8 in itself constituted just satisfaction.

50. In reaching the aforementioned decision, the Court took into account the change in the law which had been effected with regard to Northern Ireland in compliance with the Court's judgment of October 22, 1981 (Series A no. 59, pp. 7 - 8, paras. 11 - 14). No similar reform has been carried out in Ireland.

As in the Marckx case, it is inevitable that the Court's decision would have effects extending beyond the confines of this particular case, especially since the violation found stems directly from the contested provisions and not from individual measures of implementation. It will be for Ireland to take the necessary measures in its domestic legal system to ensure the performance of its obligation under Article 53 (Series A no. 31, p. 25, para 58).

For this reason and notwithstanding the different situation in the present case as compared with the Dudgeon case, the Court is of the opinion that its finding of a breach of Article 8 constitutes adequate just satisfaction for the purposes of Article 50 of the Convention and therefore rejects this head of claim.

B. COSTS AND EXPENSES

51. In respect of the proceedings before the national courts, the Supreme Court awarded the applicant taxed costs in the amount of IR£75, 762.12 (see paragraph 24 above). He submitted that this amount did not in fact fully cover the actual expenditure incurred.

The Court cannot accept this head of claim. The costs having been assessed by a Taxing Master in accordance with the law of Ireland, it is not the Court's role to reassess them.

52. The applicant also sought an amount of IR£14, 962.49 for cost and expenses, details of which he furnished, in respect of the proceedings conducted before the Convention institutions.

Whilst not contesting that the applicant had incurred additional liabilities over and above the amounts received by him by way of legal aid, the Government claimed that the legal costs sought by him were not reasonable as to quantum and required reassessment. The Court notes, however, that the Government made no counter - proposal as to what might constitute a reasonable amount.

The Court considers that the amount claimed satisfies the criteria laid down in its case-law (see among other authorities the Belilos judgment of April 29, 1988, Series A no. 132, pp. 27-28, para. 79) and awards to the applicant, in respect of costs and expenses, IR£14, 962.49, less 7,390 French francs already paid in legal aid.

FOR THESE REASONS, THE COURT

1. Holds by eight votes to six that the applicant can claim to be victim within the meaning of Article 25 of the Convention;
2. Holds by eight votes to six that there is a breach of Article 8 of the Convention;
3. Holds unanimously that Ireland shall pay to the applicant, in respect of legal costs and expenses, the amount of IR£14, 962.49 (fourteen thousand nine hundred and sixty-two Irish pounds and forty-nine pence) less 7,390 (seven thousand three hundred and ninety) French francs to be converted into Irish pounds at the rate applicable on the date of delivery of this judgment;
4. Dismisses unanimously the remainder of the claim for just satisfaction.

Done in English and in French, and delivered at a public hearing in the Human Rights Building, Strasbourg, on October 26, 1988.

Signed: Rolv Ryssdal
President
Signed: Marc - André Eissen
Registrar

In accordance with Article 51 para. 2 of the Convention, Rule 52 para. 2 of the Rules of Court, the dissenting opinion of Mr Valticos, joined by Mr Gölcüklü, Mr Matscher, Mr Walsh, Mr Bernhardt and Mr Carrillo Salcedo concurred, is annexed to the present judgment.

Initialled: R. R.
Initialled: M. A. E.

DISSENTING OPINION OF JUDGE VALTICOS APPROVED BY JUDGES GÖLCÜKLÜ, MATSCHER, WALSH, BERNHARDT AND CARRILLO SALCEDO

(Translation)

I find myself unable to concur with the majority of the Court which held that the applicant must be considered a 'victim', within the meaning of Article 25 of the Convention, of a breach of rights guaranteed by Article 8.

In fact, the applicant was not subjected to any action, penalty or other measure by his country's authorities in respect of any homosexual acts committed by him. The criminal law, in this matter, or Ireland was not enforced against him and, more generally, no prosecutions for homosexual activities in private between consenting adult men have been instituted for a number of years. The various minor difficulties of which the applicant complains were not caused by the authorities. Nor, moreover, has the applicant encountered any problems on account of the campaign which he has been overtly conducting since 1971 in favour of homosexual rights.

This case does, indeed, bear great similarities to the Dudgeon case which the Court considered that there had been a breach of the Convention. However, an appreciable and, in my view, decisive difference between the two cases lies in the fact that, in the Dudgeon case, the applicant had been subjected by the police to certain intrusions into his private life whilst, in this case, no action was taken against the applicant by the authorities.

The natural meaning of the word precludes a person from being regarded as a 'victim' of a legal provision if that person has not been subjected to any penal or other measure based on the legislation in question. The fear of prosecution which the applicant may have experienced and the psychological problems which may have been there by occasioned do not themselves suffice for a finding that the applicant is a victim. Moreover, the likelihood of the applicant's being prosecuted seems minimal regard being had to the aforementioned practice of the authorities and to the fact that the applicant has spoken out publicly on the subject of his proclivities and activities for a number of years without attracting any prosecution.

Certainly, it can never be ruled out that law regarded as having fallen into *desuetude* may one day be implemented anew. But that is not the issue here. The case turns rather on whether the applicant was in fact personally a victim. It cannot really be said that has been, or is likely to be, the case.

The system of the Convention, as a whole, is precise and, on this point, gives rise to no ambiguity or latitude. Unlike the provision in Article 24 relating to complaints lodged by Contracting Parties, an application under Article 25 by a natural person is admissible only if an applicant can claim to be the victim of a violation by a Contracting Party of the rights secured by the Convention. For the reasons which have been stated, it cannot be said that this condition is satisfied in this case.

To interpret too widely the word 'victim' would risk appreciably altering the system laid down by the Convention. The Court might then be led, even in respect of complaints from individuals, to adjudicate on the compatibility of national laws with the Convention irrespective of whether those laws have in fact been applied to an applicant whose status as a victim would be no more than very potential and contingent. An *actio popularis* would then not be far off.

I would add that this opinion in no wise seeks to call in question authority of the Dudgeon judgment as to the merits.